Why Kids Lie

ALSO BY PAUL EKMAN

Emotion in the Human Face (with W. V. Friesen and P. Ellsworth)
Darwin and Facial Expression (editor)
Unmasking the Face (with W. V. Friesen)
Facial Action Coding System (with W. V. Friesen)
Face of Man
Handbook of Methods in Nonverbal Behavior Research (co-editor with Klaus Scherer)
Approaches to Emotion (co-editor with Klaus Scherer)
Telling Lies

Why Kids Lie

How Parents Can
Encourage Truthfulness

---

by *Paul Ekman*
with Mary Ann Mason Ekman & Tom Ekman

Charles Scribner's Sons   New York

Charles Scribner's Sons
Macmillan Publishing Company
866 Third Avenue, New York, NY 10022
Collier Macmillan Canada, Inc.

Library of Congress Cataloging-in-Publication Data
Ekman, Paul.
    Why kids lie : how parents can encourage truthfulness / by Paul
Ekman, with Mary Ann Mason Ekman and Tom Ekman.
        p. cm.
    ISBN 0-684-19015-X
    1. Truthfulness and falsehood in children. 2. Child rearing.
    I. Ekman, Mary Ann Mason. II. Ekman, Tom. III. Title.
    BF723.T8E45 1989
    649'.7—dc19   88-37176 CIP
    EKM

Macmillan books are available at special discounts for bulk purchases for sales promotions, premiums, fund-raising, or educational use. For details, contact:

Special Sales Director
Macmillan Publishing Company
866 Third Avenue
New York, NY 10022

10 9 8 7 6 5 4 3 2 1

Printed in the United States of America

For Eve—may she pursue the truth

CONTENTS

Why Kids Lie

INTRODUCTION

The High Stakes of Lying

"My son Billy lied to me and he's only five. Is that normal?"

"I know Joanne is lying when she tells me she doesn't smoke pot, but I can't prove it. What should I do?"

"Michael lies all the time. Will he outgrow it?"

"Heather won't tell me what she does on her dates. She says it's none of my business, but don't I have a right to know? I'm only trying to protect her."

"When my kid lies, I worry that there's something I'm doing that makes her lie."

These are concerns common to all parents. They take on dramatic impact when someone comes to you and says: "My daughter had a great time at your son's party last week. She said you and Mary Ann were the perfect chaperons—nobody saw you!"

That's how I learned that my stepson, Tom, then thirteen years old, had lied to me. He had apparently thrown a party one summer night at our cabin in Inverness, a rural community forty miles up the coast from our home in San Francisco. I quickly surmised the party must have occurred when both my wife, Mary Ann, and I had to spend a night in the city attending to business.

Tom knew parties were supposed to be chaperoned. The parents in Inverness had made that perfectly clear to the kids. Especially after we found out some children had been drinking at an unchaperoned party the summer before. We wanted to avoid any repetition of that incident.

A few weeks earlier I had encouraged Tom to give a party. "Your mother and I will be fairly invisible chaperons," I promised him. "We'll stay out at the studio." The studio is fifty yards from the cabin, behind some trees. Tom had given a noncommittal nod of his head, and I forgot about it.

As I pieced things together, the mother who had been thanking me now looked quizzical. "There *was* a party, wasn't there?" she asked, hoping for reassurance. Frankly, I was stunned and embarrassed. "Oh yes," I mumbled and walked away. The hurt, disappointment, and anger came to me a few moments later. And, much later, came amusement.

Here I was, supposedly one of the world's leading authorities on detecting lies—in the midst of writing a book on kids and lying, no less—deceived by my own son! I thought about how foolish I would look to my friends. I was embarrassed that I was embarrassed. Later I was even more embarrassed that I had lied to the mother when I implied I knew about the party.

Just a year before this incident, I had published *Telling Lies,* an in-depth study about adult lies, based on twenty years of research. Though Tom had not read the book, he was quite aware of my expertise and, in fact, watched with pride when I appeared on TV talk shows promoting it. He knows I am an expert in spotting when someone is lying by reading facial expressions, gestures, or voice changes. He once reported that his friends had said it must be hard living with a dad who would be able to catch any lie. They wanted to know if he ever tried to get away with a lie. Tom told us he said it wasn't worth it.

But now, apparently, it had been. I wondered whether one of his motives had been to test his powers, to see whether the old man was really as good as reputed. After all, Tom was just entering his teen years, a time when a youngster needs to express his or her separateness from parents. It's an old theme between fathers and sons, and mothers and daughters.

Tom's lie may not seem like a major infraction to most parents.

Even such a commonplace lie, however, raises significant questions in a parent's mind.

Beyond not knowing what to do with, for, or to a child who lies, many parents are confused about how to react. We swing from anger to guilt, from denial to responsibility, from wanting to punish the child to wanting to ignore the lie altogether.

Mary Ann and I were very upset about Tom's secret party. We were also shocked, not by the magnitude of the lie but by its implications. Tom had always been a very reliable child. We used to brag that when he said he'd be home by six P.M., he was. We trusted him implicitly. It just wasn't like Tom to lie. Why the sudden change?

After the initial shock and anger, my feelings of being betrayed turned to disappointment. Then I began to blame myself for Tom's lie. Was it my fault for giving him too much responsibility, for letting a thirteen-year-old stay by himself overnight? Did his deceit, so elaborately planned and implemented, mean that I had failed as a parent? I must have done something wrong, maybe a lot of things, for my son to deceive me, I thought. It took a long while to sort out his responsibility from mine.

At first I was tempted to trap Tom. He had fooled his mother and me, sneaking behind our backs, and the desire to retaliate was immense. Now I had the upper hand. He didn't yet know we knew. I thought of testing him, finding out whether he would lie to my face. I could pose a question: "Say, Tom, what did you do last Wednesday night when your mom and I stayed in the city?" I could put a little more pressure on him by asking, "Tom, was anyone else at the house last Wednesday night?" Should I tell him everything I knew so he wouldn't try to lie his way out of it? If the issue of children and lying had not been so prominent in my mind, I might have reacted differently. I probably would have acted more from anger than reason, seeking revenge rather than trying to reinforce truthfulness in him.

But "reinforcing truthfulness" is easier said than done. There are many choices, and one never knows exactly which one will produce the best result.

Just a few minutes had gone by since the mother had inadvertently betrayed Tom's deceit. I knew Tom was somewhere around, and I looked for him. He was out by the bay, tossing skimmers. I called him over. "I'm very upset," I said. I could feel the heat in my face, and I struggled to keep my temper. "I just learned you gave a party behind our backs last week and lied to me about it."

He looked stunned, and seeing the guilt and panic on his face took away my anger. I suddenly felt sorry for him and for me, for I remembered in that moment what it was like to be his age and caught in a lie. "I don't want to talk to you about it tonight," I told him in an even voice. "I need time to think it over, but this is very serious. I want you to think about it, and to be ready to explain tomorrow morning what you did and what you think your mother and I should do about it."

I knew from past experience that Tom is the type of kid who always concocts the most severe draconian penalties for his misdeeds—worse than any his mother and I could ever come up with. I thought it would be good for him to worry about it and to consider what it meant. It would also give me time to think it through and be more certain that my anger would not return.

The next morning, after discussing it with my wife the night before, we grounded him for a month, barring him from going out at night or meeting his friends. We told him that since we could no longer trust him, we could not allow him again to stay alone overnight. The rest of the summer, whenever I had to spend a night in the city, I would not leave him alone at the Inverness cabin. Instead, he had to drive to San Francisco with me and then drive back the next day. That was boring for him, but the real crunch came in the fall when Tom got heavily involved in the Saturday night party scene in the city. If we were planning to spend the weekend in Inverness, in the past we would allow him to stay in the city overnight to attend a party. No longer. He had to come with us and miss the party. This loss of freedom wasn't to punish him; it was the simple consequence of his actions. Of course, it was an important lesson for him, more important than the punishment of being grounded. He learned how hard it is to live with people when they don't trust you. It was hard for us, too.

At this writing—more than two years after that incident—for the first time we have again trusted Tom to stay alone overnight. He is older now, and we have gone over this incident many times. Whenever something has come up that he might be tempted to lie about, I have been very careful about questioning him in a way that would encourage him to be truthful. Not "Who broke the vase?" or "Did you break the vase?" But "We shouldn't have kept that vase in such a vulnerable spot; it would be easy to knock it over. Was it you or your sister?"

I have made more of an effort to get him to understand why he shouldn't have secret parties, why it is important that there be chaperons for a group of kids. Sometimes I remind him of an incident that happened about six months ago. Tom had a group of friends visiting him on a Saturday afternoon. Mary Ann and I had to go to the store, and we took our daughter, Eve, with us, leaving Tom and his friends by themselves to play Ping-Pong and watch TV. We got home a few hours later, opened the front door, and were greeted by the stench of gas fumes. The top floor was full of noxious and dangerous gas. After we had quickly opened all the doors and windows and safely evacuated everyone, we found out that Tom and his friends had roasted marshmallows in the fireplace. Except when they lit the gas log, they didn't know you have to open the chimney flue to let the gas and carbon dioxide escape. An innocent mistake, but it could have been very costly.

I think this incident convinced Tom of how easy it is for a group of kids playing alone to innocently get in trouble, and why it is important to have parents around. Before allowing Tom to stay home alone overnight, I made certain he understood that this was an important test of whether we could trust him again. Without my having to tell him, he also knew that if he broke our trust once more, there wouldn't be another chance.

Lying is one of the crucial issues in family life. Imagine how complicated and awkward it would be if we could never trust that people meant what they said. It would be impossible if we had to check and verify everything we were told. We have to take people at their word—until, that is, we discover a lie. Then we learn not to trust. That knowledge can play havoc in intimate relationships. What if you worried about the truthfulness of every remark made by your child, friend, or spouse? "Can't make it home till late tonight, have to get some work out at the office." (Is she or he having an office affair?) "My homework is all done." (Is it really done, or is it time to watch "The Cosby Show"?)

It's not that everyone always tells the truth, or that we always need to know it. Politeness often requires some fabrication. "That was a delicious meal—I'm just too full for seconds," says the dinner guest even when the hostess is not a very good cook. "Sorry we can't make it, just can't get a baby-sitter," the neighbors apologize when the real reason is they want to avoid what is expected to be a dull evening. Tact often requires evasion, embroidery, and sometimes saying something that is completely untrue.

The late Professor Erving Goffman, one of the leading American sociologists, saw all of social life as a performance in which we each play the roles required and expected of us. From his perspective, no one really ever tells the truth, and it is not the truth that matters. What matters is that we follow the mostly unwritten rules of social life. I agree with Professor Goffman. Someone may show he or she cares about you by not being truthful, sparing your feelings. Sometimes the untrue message is the one that lets us know what someone is going to do. When I ask my secretary "How are you?" in the morning, I don't really want to know that she is feeling miserable because she had a terrible fight with her son. I want to know that she is going to be able to do her job well, which she assures me when she lies and says, "Just fine."

There are exceptions, instances in which someone isn't just playing out a social role but committing an outright lie, moments when you trusted that you would be told the truth and weren't. If you knew the person was lying to you, you would act differently, make different plans, evaluate the person differently. What that person gains or loses by lying is not trivial to you or to him. The stakes are usually high. When you discover such a lie, you feel violated. It hurts. It betrays your trust. Professor Goffman called these "bald-faced lies."

Bald-faced lies betray and corrode closeness. They breed distrust and they can destroy any intimate relationship. Parents can't properly fulfill their role in protecting, advising, and guiding their children if they have incorrect or false information. And yet, we all know that sometimes our children do lie to us. After all, many of us can remember lying to our parents when we were children.

What are we to do as parents? How can we preserve trust and encourage truthfulness, without being invasive, and allow our children privacy and autonomy as they grow? We don't want to make a federal case out of every lie, but neither do we want to encourage lying by ignoring it. We don't want to be such an easy mark that we tempt our child to lie, but we don't want to be so distrustful that we are suspicious of our children when we should trust them.

These are tough questions, with no easy answers. Despite the important role that lying plays, very few people have given serious thought to its nature. Few people have thought much about lying, and why and when they lie. Most of us lie much more than we think we do, and we think even less about what influence our lying may have on our children. Most parents are caught unprepared when they are faced with their child's first serious lie.

I have been studying lying professionally for more than twenty years, but it was not easy to deal with it as a parent. I have studied or thought about lies between doctor and patient, husband and wife, job applicant and employer, criminal and policeman, judge and witness, spy and counterspy, politician and voter, but only recently between parent and child. My previous study of lies focused on finding clues to deceit, telltale signs in face, body, or voice that betray a liar. Based on careful analysis of thousands of hours of videotapes of interviews with adults, I developed a theory to explain how lies differ, why some lies fail while others succeed, and whether lying is always wrong.

My interest in children's lies was sparked after *Telling Lies* was published. On call-in radio and TV talk shows promoting the book, I was confronted with a multitude of questions from parents for whom I had few good answers. They were compelling questions, and the emotional intensity in the parents' voices bespoke a deep concern, and a deeper frustration. Their questions were ones I was just beginning to face with my own children, and after my first experience of floundering live on the air, I went to the library and checked all the popular books about parenting. To my surprise I didn't find more than a page or two on lies. I could find no book specifically on children and lying, and no book written for scientists or the general public more recently than fifty years ago.

There is a bit more on children's lies in the technical scientific journals, but given the importance of this topic in family life, there isn't that much. Reading that literature I found some answers, but no one had pulled them together to help guide a parent.

To fill in some of the gaps, I and my colleague, Dr. Maureen O'Sullivan, professor of psychology at the University of San Francisco, interviewed about sixty-five children at a local school. I also interviewed more than fifty parents and almost all of my friends and colleagues who have children.

Most of the studies on kids' lies have relied on what parents and teachers say. I wanted to find out what kids say. In particular I wanted to ask them, "Why do you lie?" I wanted to present them with some moral dilemmas involving lies and see if they had thought about them. I wanted to discover their attitudes regarding lying to protect another person, lying out of peer loyalty. I also wanted to find out at what age they thought they were getting away with their lies.

Talking one to one with children was fun. For most of them, their first reaction was surprise. Nobody had ever asked them to talk about lying in a setting in which they were guaranteed anonymity and were assured they would not be reprimanded. Nonetheless, even though I assured them no one would know who they were (using a lap-top computer, I showed them how their interviews were being filed under a number, not a name), I can still not be sure their responses were not censored. They were relatively forthcoming, though, considering they were telling an adult something that they feared they would get punished for if they told their parents.

This was not my first encounter with children as subjects. I have been a school psychologist, and I've done psychotherapy with neurotic and schizophrenic children. In 1967 I interviewed children in New Guinea while researching the universality of facial expressions. In the early 1970s I was one of a dozen social scientists commissioned by the U.S. Surgeon General to conduct a one-year study of the effects of TV violence on kids.

To write this book I draw on my more than twenty years of research on the subject of lying; on my analysis, integration, and synthesis of the scientific writings I could find; on our own interviews, which filled in gaps and provided rich material for additional consideration; and on my experiences as a parent. This book is for my fellow parents. It's also for my fellow scientists, who I hope will be challenged to do more research on children and lying.

This is a family book, written for families by a family. Every member of our family contributed to it. In many ways we are a typical family; in some ways we are not so typical.

Mary Ann Mason Ekman and I are two working parents, she in her mid-forties, me in my mid-fifties. For both of us, this is not our first marriage. Tom's father died when he was eight, two years after Mary Ann and I married. That same year our daughter, Eve, was born. She is now eight years old.

Our life is hectic, typical of most families. Since we're older, we are more settled and established in our careers, not so preoccupied by our work, and at a point in our lives where we can spend more time with our children. Mary Ann and I have both gone through the personal, cultural, and political storms of earlier times, and have come back to fairly traditional values. Family is our primary commitment; work is second. We rarely work at night, hardly ever on weekends. We share child care fairly equally. In raising two children with her, I have relied often on Mary Ann's better judgment. She has not always been right (who can always be right?), but she always looks at issues from a thoughtful perspective.

In terms of discipline, you could characterize our styles as complementary. Mary Ann is more laissez faire; I'm more traditional. But there are times when we switch roles. Typical of other same-sex parent-child interactions, Mary Ann is tougher with Eve, and I'm harder on Tom. Neither of us ever uses physical discipline. Overall we're a good balance.

On the issue of lying, our ideas have changed considerably in the last couple of years. We're both more careful and conscious about how we model truthfulness to our children.

Although my daughter, Eve, couldn't write a chapter, her life offered examples and insights about lies and truthfulness in young children.

Because parents so often find it difficult to understand how an adolescent thinks about lying, I asked Tom to contribute a chapter. The only stipulation was that he be honest. Besides his own thoughts and feelings, he includes some of the comments of the friends he interviewed. His adolescent's-eye view of why kids lie is interesting, candid, and surprisingly well written—if a proud father says so himself. Talking directly to parents, Tom offers some advice about what to do when you catch your kid lying.

Mary Ann's two chapters bring to bear her early experience as a professor teaching American social history and, more recently, as an attorney dealing with divorce and custody. Her own book, *The Equality Trap* (Simon and Schuster, 1988), examines the plight of women and children in America today. In this book Mary Ann gives advice on how to respond when you know or suspect your child is lying. Her suggestions, which combine her ideas and mine, are based in part on my analysis of the scientific literature. They also draw from her historical perspective, her legal work with families in crisis, and our joint personal experience as parents.

In the last few years children have been asked to testify in court about very serious matters—from cases where their custody is in dispute, to criminal charges of child abuse, to situations in which children have testified against their own parents in drug-related charges. Their reliability as witnesses has been questioned by lawyers and judges as well as the general public. Mary Ann draws on her expertise as a family law practitioner to explain the dilemmas and controversies that surround the child in court.

In the chapters I wrote, I have drawn upon my own thinking about lying, as well as the existing scientific literature, the interviews I conducted, and my experiences with my children.

Had Tom really *lied* to me? He certainly had been sneaky in concealing the party, but he had not said anything untrue to me. Tom knew he had done something wrong, but he protested that he didn't think it was a lie. I do. There are differences between concealing the truth and saying something that is false, but I still think they're both lies, as I'll explain. I also elaborate the differences between white lies, tricking, and serious lying. It's easy to say that all lies are bad, but most parents don't treat all lies equally. They don't want their children to be truthful about everything—a tattletale is not praised, and neither is tactless truthfulness. How is the line drawn between a good lie and a bad lie, and who draws it?

Some parents inadvertently may encourage their children to lie by example. Some children are like sponges, soaking up whatever they see and hear. They also love to point out their parents' hypocrisies:

> "Why was my cheating on the test at school any more wrong than what you and Mom do on your income tax returns?"

> "You just lied to that salesperson on the phone, Mom! Why didn't you tell the truth instead of saying we were on our way out the door?"

But inappropriate modeling by parents is only one of the factors to consider in understanding why some kids lie more than others. A child's intelligence, personality, adjustment, and friendships all play a role, as I will explain.

Could Tom have gotten away with it if not for the mother who told me about his party? As an expert in spotting the clues to deceit, could I have caught Tom on my own without any help? Do you need to be an expert to spot a child's lie, or can any parent do it if he or she wants to? More importantly, should parents be spending time playing detective or counterspy when they should be spending time being good parents?

I explore this question, as well as explain why kids lie better as they get older.

I have tried to make it clear when my opinions are those of a psychologist, when they are based on solid research, and when they are based on my experience as a parent. Rather than simply report the findings, I invite the reader to explore them with me, to participate in the process of evaluating the material. You may not always agree with my choices and suggestions, but you will know what the alternatives are and at least be armed with enough information to decide for yourself.

As will become clear, the answers are not all in. A lot more research needs to be done, which will take time. But as a parent, I don't have the time to wait. I need to know now what to do with my daughter and son. In the meanwhile, offered here is one informed family's workbook on options and alternatives in dealing with children and lying. We hope that it will help parents be better prepared to implement programs that advocate honesty—and, ultimately, bring parents and children into closer, more trusting, more loving relationships.

CHAPTER ONE

Fibs, Tricks, and Boasts: The Shades of Meaning and Motivation in Lying

"THE MOST SERIOUS LIE I'VE EVER TOLD?" JACK, A SEVENTH-grader, repeated my question, looking away. After a long pause he looked right at me and spoke. "You really mean it, my parents won't find out what I say?"

"No, they won't," I said. "This is a confidential research interview just between you and me. Remember, when we began I didn't even write down your name."

I was telling him the truth. Jack is a fictitious name, since I did not record this boy's (or any other child's) real name. To be certain his parents can't identify him if they should read this book, I've also changed a few of the particulars in his account to me.

"I am trying to learn what kids think about lying," I continued. "We know a lot about what parents think about it, but not much about what kids think and do. That's why I am interviewing you and other kids in the first, seventh, and eleventh grades."

Jack looked away as he began to speak, only occasionally glancing at me as I wrote down what he said. "I was walking through the den, and I knocked the keyboard to my dad's computer off the table. I knew he'd be real mad; he's crazy about that computer. So, I put it back where it was and didn't say anything. The next day my dad said, 'Was anyone monkeying with my computer? I can't get it to work.' I didn't say a word. He asked my brother, and he said no, and then he asked me. I said, 'No I didn't touch it.' "

Jack misled his father just as Tom had misled us about the secret party he had thrown on the night his mother and I weren't home. Jack actually said something false—"I didn't touch it"—while Tom didn't have to say anything untrue to mislead us. He could fool us just by concealing.

There are many kinds of lying, just as there are many variations of the truth. The reasons people lie can range from wanting to avoid punishment to wanting to protect privacy. We can examine how lies differ from several vantage points. We can look at the technique the child used to accomplish the lie. We can examine the motive behind why the child chose to lie. We can take the perspective of the target of the lie, examining whether the target was trusting or suspicious. Or we can consider the impact of the lie, and the harm it did to the target, the liar, or someone else. These perspectives are intricately intertwined, and we will need to consider all of them to understand how lies differ.

IS THERE A DIFFERENCE BETWEEN CONCEALING AND LYING?

Some people would say that Jack lied and Tom didn't, but I think there isn't much difference between saying something false and concealing the truth. Both are lies. The purpose is the same—to deliberately mislead. If there had been a history of trouble with that computer, Jack's father might not have thought of asking his kids if they had been monkeying with it. Jack wouldn't have had to say anything untrue. Like Tom, Jack could have concealed without having to falsify. If Tom had been less scrupulous in cleaning up the party remains, he would have been in the same spot as Jack. I might have asked, "Tom, what are all these paper cups and plates doing in the garbage?" Tom would have had to say something untrue, if he was clever enough to think up an answer on the spot. (Professional liars, incidentally, don't leave such matters to chance. They prepare their answers ahead of time, memorizing a credible reply for each and every question they think their quarry might raise.[1]

Our interviews with children found that most of them do recognize that concealing the truth is a form of lying, as evidenced by their reaction to the following story that we told:

> Robert [Jane, if it was a girl we were asking] had played with his parents' stereo, even though his parents had told him not to touch the stereo if they were not around. Without meaning to, Robert broke the stereo and was afraid he would be punished when his parents found out. When his parents came home they turned on the stereo and it did not work. That night at dinner they asked, "Does anyone know what happened to the stereo?" and they looked directly at Robert, but Robert didn't say anything.

At the end of the story we asked them if they thought the child lied by not saying anything when the parents asked who broke it. Seventy percent of the kids, in both first grade and eleventh grade, said it was a lie.

Concealing is no more justifiable, no more moral or proper than falsifying.* They are just different techniques for lying. Which technique a liar chooses depends upon what the circumstances require. Everyone, child or adult, prefers to conceal the truth rather than say something false. It's easier. The concealer doesn't have to remember or defend a false line. And concealing doesn't seem as bad. It feels worse to both liar and target alike to be the victim of a false statement ("You lied right to my face!") than a concealment. Falsifying takes lying a step further than concealing. It is harder to back out. With concealment, the liar can think (or, once caught, claim) that she was

---

*The philosopher Sissela Bok makes the contrary argument, that concealing is more justifiable than falsifying, in her book *Secrets*.

about to confess and wouldn't have lied if challenged directly. That might even be true.

Tom doesn't agree with me. He does not think he lied about the party. To him lying means saying something false, while concealment is not a lie. I have challenged him on this, pointing out that since he knew he was required to tell us if he had a party, we didn't need to ask him every time we saw him, "Did you give a party?" He was obligated to report it to us. To make certain he got the point and wouldn't conceal from us again, I also used an example of getting into trouble at school. He knows if he gets into serious trouble at school—let's say, for example, the principal threatens to expel him if he gets into another fight—he has to tell us about it even if we don't ask. It's understood we don't have to ask him every day, "Did you get into any trouble at school?" All we need to do is say to him once and only once: "If you ever get into what we would consider trouble in school, you must tell us about it." Tom agrees he misled us and broke our understanding about what he has to tell us, but he still would rather not call it a lie.

LIES THAT MAY BE OKAY

Some readers may believe it doesn't matter why Jack or Tom lied. All lying is wrong, plain and simple. That's what we may conclude from the response of Vicki Frost, a thirty-four-year-old mother of four kids and a Fundamentalist Christian, who led a parents' protest against her local school board. According to *Time* magazine, ". . . she criticized materials accompanying *The Forgotten Door*, a short novel in which a child tells a lie in order to protect someone. The teacher's edition of the text suggests to instructors that they discuss in class whether a 'fib' can sometimes be a 'kindness.' Frost maintained that the Bible gives an 'absolute command' never to lie."[2]

Vicki Frost is not alone. Theologians and philosophers have argued for centuries about whether all lies are equally harmful or sinful. Many have argued that there are instances when a lie can be justified. They cite the classic example of misleading a would-be murderer who asks whether the person he is pursuing has taken refuge in your house. The argument that justifies lying is that the murderer has no right to the true information.[3] A recent study asked college students to rate the wrong-fulness of different kinds of lies on a scale ranging from 1 (if the lie is extremely wrong) to 11 (if they thought it was permissible). They found that the students rated as most permissible lies that saved others from hurt, shame, or embarrassment; and lies that protected one's privacy from an unwarranted intrusion. Lies that harmed others or that had as their sole purpose advancing one's own gain were judged as the most wrongful.[4] As they grow older, children have a more favorable attitude about altruistic lies. Most parents teach their kids to lie if telling the truth would put the child in danger. To check on what children think about this, we asked the following question:

> Imagine that you are home alone and a man who looks like a criminal comes to the door. The man asks if your parents are home, and you are afraid if you tell him the truth that he might break into the house and steal something or hurt you. So you tell him, "Yes, my parents are both home but they are taking a nap now; you will have to come back later." Is that a lie? Should you do it?

Everyone approved of this lie, but many of the younger children didn't want to call it a lie. "It's a white lie," explained one boy. "Other-wise he might hurt you." A young girl put it this way: "It's not a lie because he could hurt you, you know." Another said: "It's not a lie because they can make a fire or kill you or give your things away."

In my opinion, this is neither a white lie nor a fib. I reserve those terms for cases in which the lie is without much consequence. Telling the truth or lying to a dangerous-looking stranger about whether you are home alone has serious consequences. It is a lie, but most of us would approve of it. Many parents also approve of less serious lies, in which the lie benefits the target of the lie. For example, a ten-year-old described a lie in which she told her mother she was tired and wanted to go to bed early so she would be able to secretly make a birthday card for her mother.

CHEATING: A SPECIAL KIND OF LYING

Cheating is another type of lying children are very familiar with. In fact, when children we interviewed were asked if there were any other lies we hadn't questioned them about, they replied, "Cheating." Cheating in school is very common. Twenty-two percent of students begin to cheat in the first grade! By eighth grade 49 percent of children admit they have cheated on school assignments.[5] And it doesn't end there. In a survey of freshman high school students in California, three-quarters of them cheated on exams. Cheating may decrease by the end of high school, but the figures are still high. Thirty percent of college freshmen say they had cheated on a test in their last year of high school. When the same question was asked of college freshmen twenty years ago, only 21 percent reported cheating.[6]

When kids consider whether to cheat on a school exam, or when adults consider cheating on their income tax or on their spouse, they usually frame the issue in terms of breaking a rule, not in terms of lying. Lying is just what you have to do if you are going to cheat, a necessary function of being a thief, an embezzler, or an adulterer. Some kids think that cheating itself is not lying, but that it is lying when you deny it if challenged. In my opinion, both must be considered lies. The cheater *conceals* the real source of the information and *falsely* presents it as his own. Denying having cheated if challenged is a second lie. The denial-that-you-cheated lie is an attempt to avoid being punished, while cheating is usually an attempt to get the rewards that result from a good grade. Of course, cheating may also be an attempt to avoid punishment if the parents have made threats about the consequences of bad grades. There has been a lot of research about cheating, more than about any other kind of lie. Later I'll examine some of this research and explain what has been learned about cheating, and why some kids lie or cheat more than others.

MOTIVATIONS FOR LYING

How upset you feel when you learn your kid has lied doesn't depend so much on whether your kid concealed or falsified. Rather, the *motive* for the lie (why your child chose to lie) and the *consequences* (whom the lie affects and how) usually matter most. I believe that parents are better off when they understand why their children lie. Understanding what motivates lying may help parents decide how to respond in a way that will discourage their child from lying again. To complicate matters, there isn't one reason why kids lie; there are many. At each age group various reasons appear to be predominant, as we shall see.

Avoiding Punishment

Both Tom and Jack lied to avoid punishment. Children of every age I have studied say that avoiding punishment is the main reason why they and other kids lie. Parents and teachers also report that avoiding punishment is the most frequent reason why children lie. This is one of the most consistent findings in scientific studies of lying.

Avoiding punishment is a common motive for adult lies, too. Most thieves, embezzlers, and spies lie to conceal their acts. So does the philanderer, the job applicant who conceals being fired from his last position, and the speeder who tells the traffic cop she didn't see the 45-mph sign. They usually lie without much consideration of the morality of whether they should or shouldn't lie, or whether lying would make the consequences worse if they were to be caught. Lying is part of what they know they will have to do to avoid punishment when they decide to embark on their disapproved or illegal act. In a sense, it is wrong to say the motive for their lie is to avoid punishment. Their motive is to obtain a reward or benefit—Tom's wish to have that unchaperoned party—and lying is just part of what is required in order to get away with it. These lies are different from lies like Jack's denial that he broke the computer. One is a lie to cover an illicit pleasure, the other is a lie to conceal an unintended mistake. Success in either type of lie will avoid punishment.

When a child lies to avoid punishment, how we as parents feel about it depends on what the child did (the child's "crime," so to speak), what misdeed the child's lie hides, and, of course, the child's age. There are several things to consider:

- Is the child responsible for what he or she did? Was it a choice, made deliberately, to do something that the child knew the parents believe is wrong?
- What harm was done? Was anyone hurt? Was property damaged? Was an important principle violated?
- Did lying make it worse? If the child had not lied, would the damage have been any less?

Suppose Jack had accidentally spilled a Coke on his dad's computer keyboard instead of knocking the computer off the table. Then, not being truthful would have made the damage more costly. For if he had told his father right away before the syrupy liquid dried, the repairs to the computer might have been avoided or less costly. But that is not what happened. Jack's lie did not increase the costs of the damage he did to the computer.

Jack's misdeed was an accident. Adolescents often misjudge their body's boundaries, bumping and knocking their way around. Most people would judge Tom's misdeed (the secret party) as much worse because it was deliberate and premeditated. No one forced him to give an unchaperoned party; it didn't just happen, he chose to do it. Jack didn't intend his misdeed; Tom did.

Although less blameworthy in terms of intention, Jack's accident was much more costly than Tom's party. Fixing the computer was expensive, while Tom's party caused no damage to property or person. On balance, however, I think most people would agree that Tom's lie was worse than Jack's. Intent overrides cost in this and most instances. Tom's lie was not an afterthought, adopted to cover an unintended mistake. Lying, concealing from his parents, was part of Tom's plan from the start, when some days before the party he secretly invited his friends.

Would cheating on a school exam be worse than giving a secret party? One breaks the school's rule, the other breaks the parent's rule. I am not certain that people would agree about which, in the long run, is more problematic. Does one lead to another? Some research suggests the answer may be yes, at least with adolescents. We'll take a look at why this is so.

While Jack's dad might be aggravated by the damage done, he should hold Jack at fault for concealing, not for what he concealed. If he were to discover the lie, his dad might wonder: "Why was my son afraid to tell me? Have I acted in the past in a way which makes my son think I would punish him for an accident?" Of course, avoiding punishment might not be Jack's motive. It might be pride, a wish to avoid the humiliation of acknowledging being a clumsy, awkward teenager who doesn't know what he is doing with his body. (When he read this chapter, Tom told me this was very unlikely. "That might be the reason," he said, "if Jack broke something of his own, but if it's his dad's thing, he is going to be afraid of being punished.") I asked Jack why he didn't tell the truth. He looked at me as if I was a bit crazy for asking. He acknowledged that his dad probably would not have punished him, although he would have gotten very mad. The motive, from what I could tell, was to avoid having to bear the brunt of his father's anger, rather than fear of being punished.

I am not excusing Jack's lie, nor Tom's. I am suggesting that *parents should first determine what they think is the motivation for their child's lies. Then they will be better able to know how to deal with it.*

Avoiding Embarrassment

When Annie, a typical five-year-old, got up from her chair, her mother noticed that the seat of her pants was wet. "Annie, come over here. Are your pants wet?" her mother asked. "I didn't wet my pants, Mommy," Annie explained with great sincerity. "The chair was wet."

Annie might also have been trying to avoid punishment. But I know Annie's mother, and she would not have punished Annie for wetting her pants. Annie's lie was motivated by embarrassment. The fact that she lied shows that she has learned to be embarrassed about not controlling her bladder. The embarrassment that motivates her lie may also motivate her to learn to control her bladder. Annie's lie may also be a first step in seeking privacy, something her parents certainly claim for their own toilet functions, and something they want Annie to learn. It might not be only embarrassment. Annie might have lied so she would not have to interrupt her play. How her mom reacts—whether she punishes Annie, ignores it, or attempts to encourage her daughter to be truthful—should depend on her understanding of why Annie lied.

BEYOND TATTLING: IS YOUR CHILD AN INFORMER?

Is it right or wrong for a child to truthfully inform on someone who has done something wrong? Do you encourage your children to inform on each other for any wrong actions? Should they inform on you if you have committed a crime? Most people have not thought through their position on these matters, and there is little consensus in our society about the morality of informing. Children get mixed messages at best. On the one hand their parents discourage lying. But, on the other hand, telling the truth is not always praised by parents.

The confusion about these issues recently made newspaper headlines when thirteen-year-old Deanna Young informed on her parents for using drugs. She had attended a lecture by a deputy sheriff who spoke at the local church about drug usage. When her father and mother ignored her pleas to stop using drugs, she brought the police a bag containing marijuana, pills, and $2,800 worth of cocaine. The parents were arrested, Deanna was placed in a children's shelter, and six-figure offers from television and movie companies poured in. Ten days later

Deanna was returned to her parents, who had entered a counseling program. Within a month there were four other reports of children informing police of their parents' use of drugs.

An article on the editorial pages in the *New York Times* about the moral issues raised by this case asked, "Is the damage to the fabric of that family balanced by the public good served by confiscating a modest amount of drugs and by the message such action sends to the public? . . . Informing in a democratic society, particularly when it involves minors or family members, offers us a queasy moral paradox."[7] Taking the other side, the district attorney who prosecuted Deanna's parents said, "I admire the girl."[8] The California state superintendent of public instruction and the attorney general of California both said they sympathized with Deanna turning in her parents, calling it "a sign of success" of the school's drug education program.

My interviews with parents suggest that most of them have not talked with their children about whether it would be right for their children to inform on their parents' transgressions. Should their kid inform one parent about the other's sneaking a cigarette, flirting, or getting a speeding ticket? While parents tell their kids not to be tattletales, they do expect their kids to inform on the misdeeds of their siblings when their parents demand the information.

Trying to make sense of how I feel about this as a parent, I have come up with the following principle: Tattling is wrong when the child takes the initiative to inform, when the offense reported is minor and the motive appears to be spite. When the offense is great—if my daughter, Eve, discovered that my son, Tom, was smoking pot—I would no longer think it was wrong for Eve to take the initiative to inform me. But *she* might. Eve, who is now eight, has learned from her brother and her classmates that "telling on your brother" is wrong. She would be quite torn. So would I. If I suspected she had such information about a serious offense, I would have to balance the costs of persuading her to violate her loyalty to her brother against not knowing for certain if Tom was using drugs. Fortunately, I have not faced that impasse. However, I have faced a situation in which I think one of my children lied to cover a minor problem.

One evening Mary Ann and I went out to dinner and a movie, leaving Tom to baby-sit his sister. We told him to be certain Eve got to bed by nine, since it was a school night. The next morning at breakfast Eve was dragging herself around, obviously tired. Suspecting she had stayed up to see the end of some TV program, I asked her if she was up past nine. She denied it. So I asked Tom, "Did Eve stay up beyond nine?" He replied, "Not that I know." I can't be certain, but let's assume Tom was lying, that he knew Eve stayed up until ten. I can't see trying to punish him or her, or pushing it any further because I want Tom to feel loyalty to his sister. I want him to protect her, not be a tattler. What I could learn by getting the truth isn't important enough to try to undermine his loyalty to his sibling.

Even when the offense reported involves death, parents and their children may disagree about whether being an informer is right or wrong. That happened in an incident of racial violence in 1987 in the Howard Beach neighborhood of New York City. A twenty-three-year-old black man was struck and killed by a passing car when, attempting to escape a group of white teenagers who were attacking him with a baseball bat, he jumped onto a highway. One of the boys, Bobby Riley, provided the information that enabled the state to secure indictments against eleven other suspects. Here is the *New York Times*'s report of adults' reactions to Bobby Riley's testimony.

> A few neighbors of Mr. Riley said they believed that he and his family felt impelled by moral considerations to help the authorities. "I think it's being Catholic, that's what made him finally do it," said a [neighbor]. Another neighbor . . . said his parents must have felt it was the right thing to do.
>
> "If it was my son [who had been part of a gang attacking a black man with a baseball bat], if I didn't kill him myself first, I would like him to do whatever he could to make amends," she said.

Now listen to the teenagers.

"He did the wrong thing," said Gary Wagner, 15, a sophomore at John Adams. "You shouldn't rat on your friends, and he better move to Florida."

"Bobby Riley has no more friends—he's a stool pigeon and put my name under that," said Jody Aramo, 16, a junior.

"This is my best friend," said a girl outside John Adams High School, hugging another girl who, like her, had wavy brown hair and was wearing a blue-jean jacket. "No way would I ever rat on her, no matter what. Your friend is your friend. Do you want your friend to spend life in prison?"

The *Times* article concludes: "For the moment, for most teenagers in Howard Beach, the lessons of this case appear to have much more to do with what they consider the sin of perfidy than with any virtues in telling the truth."[9]

In this case the conflict is not simply between loyalty to friends and moral obligations to society. Bobby Riley was not an innocent bystander. The person deciding whether to protect his friends was also guilty of the same crime. A wish to make amends or meet his moral obligations may not have been all that was on Bobby Riley's mind. He might have been hoping for a lighter sentence in return for his testimony. At the time the article I've cited was published, Riley was the only one of the twelve suspects not waiting in jail for the trial to begin.

Though Riley's motivations may have been complex, the point remains that the parents and the youths offered quite different perspectives on the issue of protecting an informer.

LYING TO PROTECT PEERS

In our interviews, we explored kids' attitudes about informing on a fellow student, when they, unlike Riley, were not co-participants in the crime. By telling the truth they had nothing to gain in terms of avoiding punishment. We asked the following question: "If a teacher asked you whether your friend broke a school tape recorder, and you know your friend did it, would you tell on your friend?"

Less than a third of the children we interviewed said they would inform on their friend. The decision wasn't easy for most of the kids. Here are a number of typical responses:

"It depends on whether it was an accident."

"Your friends are more important than a broken tape recorder."

"Was it very expensive?"

"Is someone else [an innocent person] being blamed for it?"

"Had he [the person who broke it] ever told on me?"

These children are balancing conflicting moral demands in deciding what they should do. In their own way they are trying to figure out the motivation of the wrongdoer, the extent of damage done, reciprocity and loyalty, and whether an innocent party would be hurt.

How children resolve the conflict between peer loyalty and the obligations to parents or teachers was played out one day during a history class in a middle-class junior high school. The teacher was called out of the classroom to take an important phone call. One of the students got up from his seat, walked to the front of the classroom, dropped his chewing gum into the wastebasket, and picked up seventy-five cents of the teacher's money, which was lying on a table. As he put the money into his pocket, he exclaimed, "Hey look, how about that!" and returned to his seat.

The other students in the class didn't know it, but the incident was set up by two psychologists as part of an experiment designed to examine peer loyalty. The student who took the money was what psychologists call a *confederate*, someone who follows the experimenter's instructions. Dr. Herbert Harari and Dr. John McDavid, the scientists who conducted this study, recruited two confederates to steal the seventy-five cents. The so-called high-status confederate was a student whose name came up most often when classmates were asked to list five people whom they considered worthy to represent the class at a banquet for school representatives. The "low-status" confederate was a student whose name was never mentioned. In one classroom the confederate who took the money was high status, and in the other classroom the confederate was low status.

Later, the students from each classroom were called out and interviewed either singly or in pairs by one of the psychologists. Three questions were asked: "Do you know whether someone took some change left near the teacher's desk today? Do you know who took it? If so, who took it?"

All the students who were interviewed alone told the truth. Regardless of whether the classmate who had taken the money was high or low in status, no one lied. The picture changed, however, when they were interviewed in pairs. Now, whatever they did would be known by a fellow classmate—peer pressure! When the culprit who took the money was high in status, *no one* told the truth. Everyone denied that they knew money had been stolen and denied they knew who took the money. The low-status culprit was not protected. Everyone told the truth and named him. The same results were obtained in a second experiment, in which a different type of transgression was staged.[10]

But as many parents know, some children resist peer pressure more than others. Later I will examine what we know about what makes one child buckle under peer pressure more than another.

Parents do expect children to tattle on themselves, to reveal their own misdeeds even when they know they'll get in trouble. That is what I expected Tom to do about his party. That's what I still expect him to do if he gets into trouble at school. It is not an easy request, I admit, but I hope that by knowing he has to tell us he will be less likely to engage in the troublesome behavior in the first place. Whenever I can, I also try not punishing him, or punishing him much less, when he is forthright rather than when he hides some transgression.

PLEADING-THE-FIFTH LIES

Adults are not required to incriminate themselves in a court of law, but a child cannot plead the Fifth Amendment before a jury of his parents. One way out is for the child to believe that she doesn't need to volunteer the damaging information, that she is only required to give it if you ask her directly. "Not answering is not lying," one twelve-year-old told me. Even better, she may excuse herself by believing that her mom and dad don't really want to know. That line of defense doesn't usually come into play until adolescence; and it doesn't stop then. Advice columnist Ann Landers often tells her adult audience not to confess any past infidelities, to let sleeping dogs lie.

Sixteen-year-old Betsy told me that she had never lied to her parents about having had sexual intercourse. They never asked, she said, so she didn't tell them. "Sure my mom had told me once about not doing it, and disease, and pregnancy and things, but that was a couple of years ago. And Mom never asks me, like even when I come in real late, I mean real late, she doesn't ask, she just says, 'Did you have a good time?' "

Betsy thinks her parents don't want to know about her sex life or they would ask. I couldn't find out whether Betsy is right without asking her parents, which would break her confidence. But *some* parents I have told this to say they would want to know.

If Betsy's parents really don't want to know, is she really lying by not volunteering the information? Certainly she is misleading them, and deliberately so, and therefore we have to call it a lie. But if her parents really want to be misled, then it is not a very serious lie; it's more akin to politeness. We teach kids tactfulness, which means not saying what they know is true—like, "That's a really dull present, Grandma." And we encourage them at times to say what they know is false—like, "Thanks a lot! I really wanted a tie." The reason we consider this to be tact and politeness rather than lying is *not* just because it spares the target's feelings. Many lies do that. It is no pleasure for parents to learn that their child misbehaved in school, but concealing the trouble wouldn't be tact or politeness. The child knows the parent expects to be told about such incidents. Everyone knows that, for the sake of politeness and tact, we don't always tell the literal truth. We pretend to flatter, approve, and show interest. Everyone is taught the rules early.

In lies such as Betsy's, the rules aren't so well defined, and not every parent agrees on the definition. We may believe someone doesn't want to know the truth because that makes it easier for us to do what we know they disapprove of without feeling guilty about it. If the other person has not been perfectly clear about exactly what he or she expects to be told—and parents often aren't, with their kids or each other—and there is no clear social rule everyone knows and accepts, it is easy to justify concealment lies.

I suspect Betsy's parents have conflicting feelings. Like most parents, they want to know what Betsy is doing so they can try to protect her from trouble, but they are embarrassed about talking with her about sexual activity. And they are afraid that if they discover she is having intercourse and try to stop her, she will disobey and they won't be able to control her. Given those feelings, they act in a halfhearted, tentative way, which Betsy interprets as not caring. It is easy for me to say they should plunge ahead and ask her whether she is having sex, because I don't have their conflicted feelings. If they can bear to talk to her, Betsy will know her parents care, and they may be able to advise her on more safe sexual practices, if not chastity.

LIES THAT INCREASE ONE'S STATUS: BOASTING, BRAGGING

Boasting or exaggerating is another very common lie in both kids and adults. The motive is the same: to increase one's status, to appear more important, glamorous, and exciting to others. The exaggerated account is usually interesting, and more flattering than the unadorned one. In exaggerations, there is a shred of truth that is embellished and paraded. In fakery, the claim is completely untrue—the boast is about something that never happened. Kids as well as adults may imagine a much more entertaining tale than life offers them.

A friend of mine, who is a teacher, told me about seven-year-old Samantha, who exemplifies this style of bragging. The youngest of several children in her family, Samantha exaggerated stories as a means of distinguishing herself from her other siblings, my friend concluded. One time she wore a tie-dyed shirt to school and explained to my friend that everyone in her family was going to wear shirts just like hers to her uncle's wedding, at which she was going to be the flower girl. Her uncle, she said, was blind. She also said he held three jobs. Several weeks later, at a parent conference, my friend asked Samantha's mother how the wedding went. "What wedding?" the mother replied. It turned out the uncle was moving in with a girlfriend, but he was not getting married, he was not blind, and he held one job, as an accountant. "I think she told these stories because she knew she had a gullible audience in me," my friend said.

It is hard to resist being an entertainer if you have any natural talent as a storyteller. Most people consider such lies to be trivial, fibs or white lies. They harm no one (except perhaps the liar, if he later forgets what really happened). Some people disapprove of these lies because they think lying is a slippery slope. It is often said of both children and adults that if they get into the habit of telling harmless lies, they will end up by telling serious lies that harm others. No one knows whether that is really so. On this, as on so many beliefs about lying, there is no definitive research.

LIES TO PROTECT PRIVACY

The wish to obtain or maintain privacy is another common reason why kids lie. This is especially true for older kids. Some parents lie to their children for the same reason. When an amorous or argumentative exchange behind the bedroom door is overheard, parents usually cover the truth with a false account. "That noise was nothing, your father just slipped." "No one groaned, you must have been imagining something."

"I wasn't yelling, I was just telling Mom about someone who was yelling at the boss."

Parents *do* have the option to avoid such lies, and say instead, "I can't answer that question," or "It's none of your business." That is a right few parents grant to their children. When they do, it may occur without acknowledgment, as when parents learn not to ask their adolescents certain questions so their kids won't be tempted to lie. (When Tom read this section he underlined that last sentence. "This is really important," he said.)

At some point in children's development, parents have to grant their kids the right to control access to personal information. Everyone needs to have privacy, to make their own decision about who knows what about them. The growing child's need for such privacy, and his or her independence from parental control, conflict with the parent's need to protect the child from harm.

POWER LIES

Another motive for lying, which usually is not prominent until adolescence but can appear much earlier, is to test and challenge authority. A successful lie establishes the child's power, both to the child and to the parent who suspects the child has lied but can't prove it. In younger children this may first appear in teasing or tricking. When my daughter, Eve, was four and a half years old, she began to tease me by seeing whether I was gullible enough to believe her outrageous tales. I remember well one of the first times she did this.

I had asked Eve how she liked the tunafish sandwich I had made for her lunch. It was okay, she said, but not as good as her friend Martha's lunch. Martha had a whole tunafish in her lunch, not just a sandwich. I expressed doubt. Looking at me with a sly grin, Eve said, "She really had a whole tunafish in her sandwich, Daddy."

"Come on, Eve," I replied, "it wasn't the whole fish. A whole fish couldn't fit in the sandwich."

"Yes it was," she insisted. "I saw it."

"Eve, you're lying to me," I said, my voice now a little bit louder. Her tease was beginning to work.

"I'm not lying, Dad, I'm tricking."

"What's the difference?" I asked.

"When I trick you, I tell you after that it's not true."

I was impressed at Eve's ability to make such a distinction. Her teasing, which she continues with ever greater skill at the age of eight, sometimes fools me. This gives her great delight, for being able to mislead me demonstrates to both her and me her power over me.

According to my definition of lying—deliberately misleading another person—concealing the truth is just as much a lie as saying something false, especially if the person from whom the information was concealed expected to have the information without having to ask for it.

Serious lies, as I have stated, are different from fibs or white lies, politeness, tact, tricking, boasting, or exaggeration. Telling the truth is different from tattling.

Some lies, as I have also suggested, may not be wrong, and telling the truth sometimes may be harmful. I know that putting it that simply will raise hackles for some people, but we need to remember that while most lies are damaging, there are exceptions. A lie may be the only way to protect another person from harm. A lie may seem to be the only way to claim privacy when others are intrusive. A lie may be motivated by loyalty, and sometimes preserving that loyalty properly overrides any imperative to be truthful. Lies told because the target of the lie supposedly wants to be misled may also sometimes not be serious or harmful. There are situations, of course, when the liar may prefer to think the target wants to be misled when that is not the case at all.

Telling the truth can sometimes be nasty or cruel. Tattling is often spitefully motivated. Frankness can sometimes be brutal. We laugh about how the young child sometimes says what everyone knows but is too polite to mention. The classic example of this is the fairy tale about the little boy who shouted out that the emperor wasn't wearing a new suit at all—he was naked! Adolescents may not seem at all funny when they make quite unpleasant but truthful remarks about some odd habit or unfortunate appearance defect in a parent.

To sum up, there are many different motives for lying:

- To avoid being punished
- To get something you couldn't get otherwise
- To protect friends from trouble
- To protect yourself or another person from harm
- To win the admiration or interest of others
- To avoid creating an awkward social situation
- To avoid embarrassment
- To maintain privacy
- To demonstrate your power over an authority

These are not the only motives for lying, but they are among the most common ones reported by children, parents, teachers, and experts who have studied or speculated about why kids lie. None of these motives for lying is unique to kids; they also motivate adult lies. Some of the motives, however, do become more important than others in older children.

While there are various motives, there is as much variety to the reasons why some children develop a greater propensity for lying than others. Some of it has to do with a child's personality. Some of it has to do with the environment in which the child is growing up. Some of it has to do with age.

CHAPTER TWO

Why Some Kids Lie More Than Others

AT ONE IN THE AFTERNOON JERRY, AN ELEVEN-YEAR-OLD fifth-grader in Chicago, became part of the world's largest scientific study of cheating, lying, and stealing. He and nearly eleven thousand other children from nineteen schools participated. Most of them were in the fifth through eighth grades, although there were some in grades nine through twelve. They were tempted to cheat on school tests, in athletic performances, and in playing party games. Some also had the chance to steal money.

In all, there were thirty-two different situations in which children could act honestly or dishonestly. Most children spent about four hours in the study, enough time for them to give in to or resist a number of temptations to cheat. Some of the children were asked if they had cheated. Some confessed, others lied. Dr. Hugh Hartshorne and Dr. Mark May, the psychologists who directed this classic study, also found out about the parents and home environment of some of these children.

This landmark study was sponsored by Teachers College of Columbia University, in cooperation with the Institute of Social and Religious Education. The information gathered was massive, and no scientific study of lying or cheating since has been its equal in scope or size. The amazing thing is that this gigantic study was done in the mid-1920s! Even more amazing is that so much work was done so well so long ago. Two books, published in 1928, reported the findings at length and in great technical detail. I suspect this may be why the work did not have the impact it should have had. It is a lot to digest. (The pros and cons of this fascinating study are discussed at the end of this book.)

Much of what I will explain about why some kids lie more than others was discovered by the pioneering doctors Hartshorne and May. I pay most attention to those of their findings which have been borne out by more recent research. Sometimes no one followed in their footsteps, and we only know what they discovered more than sixty years ago. There are some discoveries not anticipated by Drs. Hartshorne and May that I will also cover.

The most interesting part of their study is the differences they found between children who didn't cheat and those who cheated and denied it when challenged. There were two questions to ask. First, what distinguishes those kids who don't cheat or lie from those who do? In order to answer that, I've concentrated on three characteristics of the child: intelligence, maladjustment, and personality. I also consider outside influences: parents, friends, and home environment. As it turns out, all of these factors play a part. The second question is: If my child lies, does that mean that he or she is likely to get into serious trouble later in life? It's a good question. Before we can answer it, we need to go back to Hartshorne's and May's study. (In the following account, the names are fictionalized but everything else is factual, including direct quotes.)

When Jerry's teacher left the classroom, a woman who introduced herself as Mrs. Norman stood at the front of the class. She said, "We are going to have some tests today. When the papers are passed [out], they will be fully explained. Do you each have a sharpened pencil and an eraser? Do you have some scratch paper to figure on? This test is made up of some arithmetic problems. I will pass out an answer sheet with each test so that you can correct your own papers. The answer sheet is the typewritten sheet. Keep it under your paper and out of sight until you have finished."[1]

Jerry opened the booklet. The first question asked, "How many eggs are needed to make 3 cakes if you use 2 eggs for one cake?" He did the calculation, then wrote his answer down. Maybe I should just check to see if I am doing it right, he thought. He took a peek at the answer sheet underneath his paper. He was right.

The next question was harder: "18 equals —% of 40?" Jerry was more uncertain about how to do this one. He hesitated a moment, then looked at the answer sheet and wrote down the correct answer.

After that, every time Jerry was uncertain he looked at the answer sheet.

Mrs. Norman collected the arithmetic test. On the next test, Jerry had to figure out the words that complete a sentence like: "The poor little ——— has ——— nothing to ———; he is hungry." This time Mrs. Norman didn't give the answer sheets with the test. The temptation came later. After twenty minutes, Mrs. Norman said, "Stop and correct your papers. This is the answer sheet. It gives the correct answer for each question. Put a C after each answer that is right and an X after each answer that is wrong. Do not mark the ones you skipped. Count the Cs. That is your score. Put this number at the upper right corner of the front page."

As he corrected his paper, Jerry changed some of his answers. The next test was of general information and, as with the word completion test, Mrs. Norman gave out the answer sheet so the kids could score their own test. Jerry cheated on this test, too. On the last of the tests, the opportunity to cheat was arranged somewhat differently. "In the Word Knowledge test," Mrs. Norman explained, "you are to give the meaning of some words. You will have to take this test home and do it as part of your homework. Do the test all by yourself and do not get any help from anyone or even from the dictionary. Do it today and bring it back tomorrow. Do not get any help on it."

A few days later Mrs. Norman returned to Jerry's class. She again handed out tests very similar to the ones the group had taken before. Although they tested arithmetic, word completion, general information, and word knowledge, the questions were all different. This time there were no answer sheets, no take-home test, no chance for Jerry to cheat. This time the tests measured what Jerry actually knew. By comparing scores on the two tests, Drs. Hartshorne and May learned who cheated. Jerry did so much worse the second time that it couldn't just have been a bad day for him. Nor could it have been due to differences between the two forms of the test. Comparing the results of the first battery of tests with the second showed the scientists which children cheated.

While the scientists knew who had cheated, the cheaters did not know the scientists knew. A week later Jerry's teacher handed out a questionnaire. The questions at the beginning were quite innocent:

Do you like dogs?

Are you usually happy?

Do you feel rested in the morning?

Then came the questions to see if the cheaters would lie about it:

Do you remember taking some tests a short time ago given by a person who was not your teacher?

Do you remember taking one of those tests home with you to be done at home?

Did you actually do this test all alone, without getting any help on it?

If you did get help, was it from some person?

Or was it from a book or dictionary?

Did you understand at that time that you were not to get help in doing the test?

On some of these tests you had a key to correct your paper by. Did you copy any answer from the keys?

Forty-four percent of the kids cheated by copying on the school tests. The figures varied from a low of less than 20 percent to a high of over 50 percent, depending on the school room, the school, and the age, sex and race of the kids. These figures are probably conservative, since kids who cheated only on one or two questions would not have been detected. The great majority of that 44 percent lied when asked if they had cheated. In every grade more than half—usually more than 80 percent—of the kids who cheated then lied. Yet some 20 percent of the kids who cheated did not then lie but confessed, and there were indeed others who didn't cheat in the first place.

The question for us is: Why were some kids honest and didn't cheat, while others cheated and then lied, denying they had cheated? What are the differences between liars and honest kids?

To answer these questions, Drs. Hartshorne and May selected two groups from the thousands of children who had taken these tests. Both represented different grades and schools, and both had an equal number of males and females. The eighty children who did not cheat on any of the tests were identified as the honest group. They were compared with ninety children who did cheat and then denied cheating. On visits to the homes of most of these children, the scientist interviewed the parents and observed how they interacted with their children.

The question I asked of the Hartshorne and May study was: Were the children who lied different from the honest ones? The answer, I found, was yes and no. The liars had more disadvantages—Hartshorne and May called them "handicaps"—in their family relations, in their environment, and in their personal characteristics.

While important, the differences between the liars and honest kids were not enormous. There were some liars who had very few handicaps, no more than most of the honest kids. But some of the honest kids had as many handicaps as most of the liars. Although twenty-four different handicaps were measured—from the child's maladjustment to the income level of the parents—the findings show that these handicaps do not completely explain whether or why a child lies or cheats.

Bearing in mind that their findings won't fit every individual child, let's examine their study, with particular emphasis on those findings that have withstood the scrutiny and tests of other researchers in the nearly sixty years since its publication. We will find not one, but many factors associated with lying.

ARE LIARS LESS INTELLIGENT?

Below-average I.Q. was more common among liars than honest children. About one third of those kids with the lowest I.Q.s lied and cheated. None of those kids with the highest I.Q.s lied or cheated. Even in between these two extremes, the figures consistently show that the higher the I.Q., the lower the percent of kids who lied. As with almost all of the studies of children's intelligence in the last fifty years, smarter kids lie less.[2]

Hartshorne and May considered the possibility that socioeconomic background might play a more influential role in explaining why smart kids lie less. They knew that children from more privileged upper middle-class homes do better on I.Q. tests. They also had evidence that the cultural level in the home (the amount of art, music, and literature children were exposed to) is related to lying. To find out whether I.Q. was an important variable separate from family wealth or I.Q., they studied children in private schools who all came from similarly privileged homes. Even when the benefits of wealth could be ruled out, mainly because everyone had it, they found I.Q. was still related to cheating.

Why should smarter kids cheat less? Maybe they don't need to cheat. They know they have the intellectual prowess to get good grades without cheating or lying. If that explanation is correct, Hartshorne and May reasoned, then smart kids might cheat as much as dumb ones when tested in a situation in which they didn't think their exceptional intellectual abilities would help them. Not surprisingly, they found that cheating at party games, in athletic performances, or on tests of mechanical skills and stealing was not related to I.Q. Instead of saying kids who are smart cheat and lie less, we should specify that children who are specially talented—whatever that talent may be—are less likely to cheat when that talent is likely to ensure success. I am assuming that athletically gifted kids would be less likely to cheat when tested at that ability, but to my knowledge no one has done such a study.

Psychologist Roger Burton, who has been studying dishonesty for the last twenty-five years, put it this way: "The relationship of honesty to I.Q., therefore, was essentially limited to academic-type tests in which previous experience of failure in similar school situations led [some] low-I.Q. and low-achieving subjects to cheat. Cheating for these children had become a means of accomplishing what seemed unattainable by honest routes."[3]

Dr. Burton might be overstating the case. Success wasn't totally unattainable for all the kids who cheated and lied. The children with average I.Q.s were smart enough to do well on school tests if they worked hard at it, yet they cheated more than the kids who had higher I.Q.s. In other words, maybe they cheated to avoid having to put in that extra work. Perhaps if the bright kids, who presumably didn't have to work hard, were faced with stiffer tests requiring more study, more of them would also have cheated. From the research that exists, we can't be certain if some children cheat and lie to avoid failure or to avoid the necessity of having to work harder than some of their classmates.

There is another quite different explanation for why I.Q. might be related to lying. Hartshorne and May thought that maybe the brighter kids were more cautious, that they recognized the risks involved with cheating. While they had no way to test this idea, subsequent research by other scientists showed they were right. In an experiment reported in 1972, fifth-grade children were given school tests much like those administered by Hartshorne and May. All of them had the chance to cheat by changing their answers when scoring their tests. The experimenters set up the situation so that the risk of cheating would seem high for half the kids, while for the other half it would seem there was little chance of being caught. The results showed that for the children who thought they wouldn't be caught, I.Q. didn't matter. Smart kids cheated as frequently as less intelligent children. It was only when there was a good chance of being caught that the smarter kids didn't cheat as much as the less intelligent kids.[4]

There is still a third explanation of how intelligence might be related to not lying or cheating, an explanation not considered by Drs.

Hartshorne and May. Smart kids might just be better liars, more clever cheaters.[5] Smart kids may tell better lies that are less easily detected. This couldn't have happened in the Hartshorne and May research because they arranged the study so they would know for certain who lied. But there is no experimenter in real life. Not every liar gets caught. Parents or schoolteachers don't always know who has cheated. Unlike the mythical Pinocchio, there are no telltale long noses that tell us when our children are lying to us. Following this line of reasoning, we may infer that highly intelligent children may lie even more than others if they learn they can get away with it, and more so if they are under more pressure from their parents to achieve.

We should not think of intelligence, then, as a protection or guard against lying. If your child is above average in intelligence, that is no assurance he or she won't cheat or lie. In fact, an intelligent child may be a more skilled liar, and therefore avoid detection. It will depend on opportunity, pressure, and other factors.

Though some of the data suggests otherwise, it isn't that the smart kids understand that lying and cheating are wrong. They just don't lie and cheat when they think they will get caught, and/or when they can succeed without lying or cheating.

If your child is closer to average intelligence, there may be more temptation for him or her to cheat in school, especially if you are pushing hard on grades and the competition is stiff. That doesn't mean he or she has to cheat or lie, only that there may be more reason to consider it.

THE STORY OF JAMES: ARE LIARS MALADJUSTED?

I have known James since he was seven. That was when his mother, Alice, married Karl, one of my closest friends. His first marriage had ended four years earlier. James was a good-looking boy. He seemed to get along easily with other kids and adults, but even then his grades in school were not very good. In third grade, soon after his mother's remarriage, the teachers reported that James was lying. Karl was mortified. There was nothing that could have bothered him more than lying. To him being forthright was one of the basic tenets all people should live by; lying was the ultimate slap in the face. He talked to me about it, but I had not yet begun to study children and lying and didn't have much advice to offer.

James's lying continued. By the time he was eleven, he had stolen money from his mother's purse. He had denied that he broke one of his stepfather's cameras. He was still doing poorly at school. By fourteen James was a truant and had been caught using marijuana. In desperation, admitting their own failure, his parents sent James away to a residential school. It was not very successful. James as an adult has not held a steady job, and has appeared in court more than once for a petty crime.

Before assuming that lying as a child leads to negative behavioral consequences as an adult, consider another story—from my own life—that provides opposite evidence. I lied often as an adolescent of thirteen and fourteen, but I didn't become a truant. I was a secret cigarette smoker starting at twelve. At thirteen I discovered jazz. Living in New Jersey only an hour away from the best jazz clubs in Manhattan, I forged a driver's license, legalizing my age as eighteen. I secretly bought the clothing that befit a "jazzbo." On Friday nights I would tell my parents I was going to New York to stay at a friend's house. I would go to the bus station, where I secretly kept a locker, change out of my thirteen-year-old's school clothes, and put on my royal blue peg-legged pants, bright yellow turtleneck shirt, and maroon cardigan jacket. Thus attired, I would meet my friend in front of a jazz club. In the subdued light of the nightclub, with my costume and forged driver's license, I would gain admission to the club, where we listened to jazz and drank beer until four in the morning.

The next day I would return to the bus station and change back into my other clothes and return home. My parents never found out about my secret life, although two years later they did catch me smoking.

While I got thrown out of junior high school for talking back to a teacher, I never engaged in antisocial behavior as an adolescent or adult, and I have held the same job for more than thirty years. Now, however, like any parent, I am worried that my son, Tom, might try the same kind of tricks I pulled when I was his age.

Whose life story should we learn from, James's or mine? Are children who lie generally more maladjusted? Is lying one of the first steps on the path to maladjustment, antisocial behavior, and perhaps crime? The scientific evidence suggests the answer may be yes, for some kids.

Though Hartshorne and May found there was more maladjustment in liars than in the kids who didn't lie or cheat, the differences were small. The teachers gave lower grades on classroom deportment to a few more of the liars, and some of them scored worse on a test of neurotic tendencies. Recent research has found much more evidence that lying is related to maladjustment.

Children whose adjustment problems led them to be treated at a mental health agency were reported to lie more often than children in general. This finding comes from seven separate studies reported in the last fifteen years. The children ranged in age from five to fifteen. Looking over these studies, I found the prevalence of lying is two and one-half times higher among these maladjusted children than it is among normal children. The types of maladjustment that appear to go along with more frequent lying are conduct disorders and aggressive behavior. For example, in one study 65 percent of the children with conduct disorders were reported to be liars, as compared to 13 percent of those with neurotic problems. Children who lie are also frequently reported to use alcohol or drugs, have bad companions and belong to gangs, be stubborn, set fires, and blame others. It is not a pretty picture.

One of the largest studies[6] was a comparison of parents' comments on children who had been referred to a mental health clinic and children who didn't require such care. There were 2,600 children in all, ranging in age from four to sixteen, representing both males and females, whites and blacks, and various social classes. Half were referred for care (the "maladjusted") and half presumably were trouble free (the "controls"*).

The parents provided information about 138 different aspects of their children's behavior. One of these questions asked if their child lied or cheated often, sometimes, or not at all. Almost half of the maladjusted children were reported to lie and cheat, while only a fifth of the control children lied and cheated. There are many differences between maladjusted and control kids, but the discrepancy in lying was one of the largest. This difference in lying and cheating was found regardless of socioeconomic status, sex, or race. (It's interesting to note that feelings of sadness, unhappiness, and depression, and doing poorly in school, were areas that reflected the most marked differences between maladjusteds and controls).

Although the maladjusted kids were said to lie more than the control kids at every age, the greatest differences were at age sixteen. Nearly 90 percent of the sixteen-year-old maladjusted boys, and almost 70 percent of the sixteen-year-old maladjusted girls, were reported to lie and cheat. By contrast, less than 20 percent of the same-aged control boys and girls were reported to lie and cheat.

In the course of their research Drs. Thomas Achenbach and Craig Edelbrook found other characteristics frequently associated with maladjusted kids who lied and cheated, among them stealing, having bad friends, engaging in vandalism, and being truant. Currently one of the most active researchers in the area of lying and antisocial behavior, psychologist Magda Stouthamer-Loeber and her husband, Rolf Loeber, studied fourth-, seventh-, and tenth-grade boys from twenty-one different metropolitan school districts in Oregon.[7] They found frequent lying, as reported by parents and teachers, was associated with stealing, drug

---

*Scientists use the term "control" when they are comparing two groups for which everything else remains the same except for the characteristic they are testing. In this case, they are controlling age, sex, race and social class so that, apart from those variants, they may sort out what is associated with maladjustment and what is normally found in any group of comparable children. In this manner, they can determine what effect maladjustment has on lying.

use, and fighting. The relationship was strongest for the tenth-graders, although it was apparent also in the fourth- and seventh-grade boys. (Tenth-graders don't fight as much as seventh-graders, and therefore the relationship between lying and fighting was not as strong for the older boys as the younger ones.)

The tenth-grade boys who lied also had more contact with the police and more truancy. The relationship between lying and stealing was remarkably strong among these boys.

THE HALO/HORNS EFFECT

There is a problem with almost all these studies of lying and maladjustment, including Dr. Stouthamer-Loeber's, and that is that they are vulnerable to what psychologists call the "halo effect." That phrase refers to the fact that if you know something good or bad about a person, you are likely to think he or she will have other good or bad traits. If you were asked if Mother Teresa likes puppies, you would probably say yes. I call it the "halo/horns effect" because it can work either way, positively or negatively. Asked if Hitler liked babies, most people would probably say no. The halo/horns effect misleads us into expecting that someone bad like Hitler would not do something nice, such as liking babies.

In the classroom the halo/horns effect works this way: Suppose a teacher is having trouble with a boy who talks back, fights, steals, or doesn't listen. Even if the teacher never actually catches him lying, the halo/horns effect may lead her to think he is a liar. Even if the halo/horns effect doesn't lead her to imagine she saw him lie, it might make her watch that person more closely. Under such scrutiny it would be more likely the boy would be caught if he did lie. On the other hand, the goody-goody who causes no trouble might benefit from the positive side of the halo/horns effect. Even though such a teacher's pet might lie just as much as the troublesome child, the teacher would not be on the watch and therefore wouldn't be as likely to catch him in a lie.

Findings that rely on teachers', parents', or friends' reports of lying to determine who lied are vulnerable to the halo/horns effect. So far, all of the research on lying I have reviewed is vulnerable, except for the Hartshorne and May study. They didn't rely on a teacher's or parent's report to determine who lied; they arranged situations, tests, and games in which they could see for themselves who cheated and denied it when asked. Without the influence of the halo/horns effect possibly biasing the results, the effect is still evident but less so.

We should not dismiss these findings, however, because of the halo/horns effect. While it is not possible to estimate just how strongly lying is related to maladjustment, maladjusted children probably do lie more often than children who are not having trouble. By definition, these maladjusted children are not succeeding in their lives. They are breaking rules set by their parents, their school, and society and they are being caught in their transgressions. Children who are breaking the rules are going to lie if they want to avoid punishment for their transgressions or if they can't get what they want without lying. That's why I lied to get into the nightclub when I was underage.

DOES MALADJUSTMENT CAUSE LYING OR VICE VERSA?

All of this simply suggests that lying is a feature, not a cause, of maladjustment. Let's consider for a moment the possibility that lying actually causes a child to *become* maladjusted. This view would argue that kids who lie, and who learn they can get away with things by lying, are likely to break other rules. If they are following this path, the theory would continue, as they grow up they will engage in other wrong acts. Sliding down life's slippery slope, one wrong act will lead to another, and a youthful liar will quite possibly become a hard-core social deviant. Because they are accustomed to lying, they may be more willing to do things they know they could be punished for because they expect their lies will protect them.

· Returning to the question of whether lying is a feature of maladjustment or a cause of it, these studies don't provide enough information for us to choose between these two views. Either way, frequent lying is a danger sign. It may not be the only one. There may be other indicators of maladjustment. But if your child lies often, and this lying (not teasing or game playing) persists over an extended period, you should take it seriously. If being deceitful has become your child's normal pattern of behavior, the time has probably come to find out why. One thing to consider is whether your own actions encourage your child to lie. Are your rules too strict? Are you overprotective? Are you invading your child's privacy? Do you lie often in front of your child, conveying the message that lying is all right? Explain to your child how lying affects trust, and how hard it is for people who live together to get along without trust. Be certain your child understands that you do not accept lying and why.

THE MACHIAVELLIAN LIE: ARE LIARS MANIPULATORS?

Twenty years ago, a number of psychologists began to study people who are highly skilled at manipulating others for personal gain. Such people are not concerned with conventional morality; their concern is in power over others more than how others feel. One of these psychologists, Dr. Richard Christie, constructed a questionnaire to identify such people. Much of the questionnaire was based on ideas in Machiavelli's book *The Prince,* first published in 1513. Although Machiavelli provided advice on complex political issues, his name has come to be associated with the use of "guile, deceit and opportunism in interpersonal relations."[8] A popular book of the seventies, *Power!,* written by Michael Korda, the editor in chief of Simon and Schuster, exemplifies part of this approach to life: "Some people play the power game for money, some for security or fame, others for sex. . . . No matter who you are, the basic truth is that your interests are nobody else's concern, your gain is inevitably someone else's loss, your failure someone else's victory."[9]

Most of the research on Machiavellianism (researchers call it

"Mach" for short) has studied adults. A few investigators have examined children to see if those who scored high on Mach lied more often or more successfully. The questionnaire identifying the Mach characteristics had to be modified for younger ages, but the content is the same as with adults. Here are examples of a version used with children:

> Never tell anyone why you did something unless it will help you. (A Mach answers yes.)
>
> Most people are good and kind. (A Mach answers no.)
>
> The best way to get along with people is to tell them things that make them happy. (A Mach answers yes.)
>
> You should do something only when you are sure it is right. (A Mach answers no.)
>
> It is smartest to believe that all people will be mean if they have a chance. (A Mach answers yes.)
>
> You should always be honest, no matter what. (A Mach answers no.)
>
> Sometimes you have to hurt other people to get what you want. (A Mach answers yes.)
>
> Most people won't work hard unless you make them do it. (A Mach answers yes.)
>
> It is better to be ordinary and honest than famous and dishonest. (A Mach answers no.)
>
> It is better to tell someone why you want him to help you than to make up a good story to get him to do it. (A Mach answers no.)[10]

In the most interesting experiments,[11] forty-eight pairs of fifth-grade children were given the Mach questionnaire and then, based on their answers, separated into three groups representing high, middle, and low propensity for Mach behavior. Kids were then paired, linking a middle scorer to either a high or low Mach scorer.

When a pair of children arrived for their interview, the middle Mach child was told to read a magazine while the other child was taken into the experimental room. In the experimental room, the subject sat opposite the experimenter. On a table between them was a plate containing fifteen small bitter-tasting crackers (they had been presoaked in quinine solution). The experimenter told the subject that she was a home economist working for a cracker company. Her job was to find out what children thought about the taste of a new "health cracker" before it went on sale in stores. Upon tasting it, the child naturally found the cracker distasteful. After letting the child have a drink and a piece of candy to get rid of the offensive taste, the experimenter then said: "So far no one has eaten very many of these crackers, and I guess you can see why. But it's really important to us to know how these crackers taste after someone has eaten a few of them. You know, if a person gets used to them and doesn't mind it after a while, if they taste better the more you eat of them. Since you know [the name of the other child], maybe if you asked him to eat the crackers he might be willing to do it, being he knows you and is in your class. . . . You'll be doing me a favor, so I'll give you five cents for each one you get him to eat. . . . I really don't care what you tell him or how you get him to eat the crackers, just so long as he eats as many as possible. If you don't want to ask him, I really won't mind and you can leave now. Okay?"

The other child was then brought into the room, and their conversation was tape recorded and later analyzed. The children who scored high on the Mach questionnaire were more successful in getting the other child to eat crackers than the children who were low scorers. How did successful cracker salespeople convince other children to eat the distasteful crackers? By lying. High Mach children lied more than low Mach kids. The high Mach girls, incidentally, told more subtle lies than boys.

The high Mach kids not only misled their classmates their own age, but they also impressed adults. The experimenter asked some adults to listen to the tape recordings and rate each child on a number of different scales. The kids scoring high on the Mach test were rated as more innocent, honest, and comfortable than the kids who were low scorers. Very similar results were found by Dr. Susan Nachamie in a study of sixth-grade students.[12] She used a dice game in which the children could choose whether to bluff (asserting false claims about the value of their dice) or be truthful. Although the children could earn points by either bluffing or being truthful, successful bluffing would produce more rewards. The children who scored high on the Mach scale earned more, chose to bluff more, and succeeded at it more often than low Mach children.

A Machiavellian approach to life is less prevalent among preadolescents than it is among adolescents and adults, according to some studies. However, some preadolescents do show a manipulative orientation. Commenting on this, Dr. Christie and his collaborator, Dr. Florence Geis, said:

> ... exposure to the world outside the home leads to the fabled loss of childhood innocence and higher scores on the Mach scale [in some children] . . . Some adults score much lower on the Mach scale than the average ten-year-old and by all known criteria have maintained a trusting faith in their fellow man . . . while we have no systematic data as yet on children under ten, there is anecdotal evidence which suggests that some cherubs are very facile con artists.[13]

These findings raise an important question: What causes some children to be very manipulative? The natural place to look for an answer is in the home, and specifically at the parents. There are two possible explanations. First, the parents might themselves be manipulators, and kids simply learn this behavior. The opposite might also be possible. If the parents are low Mach, their very trustfulness might unwittingly encourage their children to develop manipulative traits, since the parents would be such easy marks. Unfortunately, the evidence is contradictory, as there are two different studies supporting opposite possibilities.[14] Perhaps both can occur.

These studies, which suggest that lying may be part of a more general manipulative personality pattern, do have one very important limit. The lies these children told were encouraged by authority figures. The experimenter asked the children to help her do her job as an economist. The children who lied did so not only to gain rewards but to help an adult who appeared respectable and responsible. The rules of the dice game made it clear to the children that they could win more by bluffing well. Bluffing by definition was allowed, if not required.

We don't know if children who lie when they are not encouraged to do so, who lie when breaking rather than following rules set down by adults or society, are high on Machiavellianism. My bet is that they are.

What should you do if you think your child is becoming a manipulator? First of all, don't panic. Get a second opinion by discussing your child's behavior with others who know him or her, such as a teacher, and see if they agree. You may be worrying too much about a transitory situation.

Are you encouraging your child to develop this trait by either being a pushover, or by being a manipulator yourself? And remember neither might be true: some children may develop manipulative tendencies regardless of how their parents act.

Most importantly, become more actively involved in the moral education of your child. Help your child understand that there is a lot more to be concerned about than having power over others.

DO KIDS LIE BECAUSE OF POOR PARENTING?

"Am I lucky! I really didn't think the policeman would believe my story about the broken speedometer. I must be a better actor than I thought I was."

This woman was so pleased at lying her way out of the speeding ticket that she didn't think about what impression she might be making on her nine-year-old son as he silently listened to her tell her husband about the incident that night at dinner.

It is not surprising that children who lie the most often have parents who also lie frequently. Hartshorne and May came to that conclusion in their study, and two other studies since then also found that kids who lie the most come from homes in which parents also lie often or endorse breaking rules.[15]

This isn't the only negative influence parents can have, but it is one parents may not readily realize. Lying to the traffic cop, fudging on income tax, giving a phony excuse for being late are such common-place deceits that they go unnoticed—by parents, that is. Some parents might be offended that I call these lies, but they are. Their purpose is to mislead and thereby avoid punishment or embarrassment, or to gain something that would otherwise be difficult to attain. Children lie for the very same reasons, and to some extent they learn to lie at home. Jay Mulkey, the president of the American Institute for Character Education, a foundation that works with teachers, said, "A child cheats on an exam and his parents get outraged. Yet he keeps hearing his folks talk about cheating on expense accounts or income taxes."[16]

Hartshorne and May also found that the children who lie came from homes in which there was less parental supervision. This was also found in a recent study of lying by fourth-, seventh-, and tenth-grade boys. Boys who lived in single-parent homes, or homes in which the parents were unhappily married, lied more. Incidentally, having both parents in the home didn't help if the marriage wasn't working. Such unhappy marriages were no different from single-parent homes, but both were worse than happily married families in terms of whether the children lied.[17]

In single-parent homes, which in most cases translates to mother and children (no father), there is less control of the kids. Mothers have the most problems with their sons, especially when they reach adolescence. Peers more easily win out over parental influence in such homes. The boys go along with their buddies, and are more prone to antisocial acts. Importantly, this finding holds up even when family income and parents' education is taken into account: there was more trouble among the offspring of mother-only households than in dual-parent families even when both groups had equally low incomes.[18]

Parental rejection is also related to lying, more so if the mother rejects the boy than if the father does. Drs. Stouthamer-Loeber and Loeber raised the chicken-and-egg question of which comes first. Maybe parental rejection doesn't cause their kids to lie; maybe the parents reject their kids because they are liars. In other words, it may not always be the environment that makes the child, but the child who determines how the environment reacts.

This in turn raises the question: Could there be a genetic factor responsible for lying? Once again Drs. Hartshorne and May provide us with some relevant information, exploring the role of heredity in lying. They found a link—a weak link, but a link nevertheless—that showed siblings lied the same amount. Since siblings share some genetic heredity, we may make some inferences about the possibility that lying may be gene-linked. The link between siblings and lying is stronger, in fact, than the link in intelligence. Even when intelligence was accounted for, there was still a relationship between siblings in how much they lied.

However, since siblings live in the same house, home environment, not heredity, could be responsible for similarities in lying. Trying to isolate the influence of heredity, Hartshorne and May studied orphans, who no longer lived at home. The correlation in the amount of lying between siblings was still evident. That is not convincing enough for me, for the orphanage is now the home environment, shared by the siblings. It would be much more convincing if they had studied orphans reared from near birth in separate, different home environments. In an orphanage siblings may have many of the same friends, and as we shall see, friendships influence lying and truthfulness.

There is no doubt that you as parents have a major influence on your children when it comes to attitudes, beliefs, and social actions such as lying or cheating. You are not the only influence, but you are a very important one. It is easy for me to suggest that you carefully consider whether you are providing a negative model by lying more than you think. It isn't easy to get out of the habit of absentmindedly indulging in small lies that make your own life more convenient.

I find it hard not to fall into the trap of lying, and I have been consciously making an effort not to do so for a number of years. A false excuse is without doubt the easiest way out of an awkward social situation, the perfect way to dodge an invitation or request I don't want to comply with.

I have learned to go through the extra step of not taking that path. When I get a telephone call from a salesperson, I say that I have a policy of not buying by phone—rather than saying I can't talk now because I have something on the stove. I make a point of talking to my kids about how to handle such situations, letting them know I have to deal with the same problem. Even as young as eight, my daughter, Eve, has no trouble understanding the conflict and the temptation to lie in such situations. For example, what should Eve say to the kid in her class whom she didn't invite to her birthday party? I described how that kid might be hurt more when she found out Eve lied to her than if Eve told her the truth. I explained how it wasn't so terrible to say that your parents had set a limit on how many kids you could invite, so you had to pick your closest friends.

What can a single parent, and particularly a single mother, do about the findings that show lying is most prevalent in such homes? And what can she do for her adolescent son, who the research shows is more prone to antisocial behavior, especially in the absence of a father? First, there is some solace in knowing you are not alone; others share the problem. Try to find a male friend or family member who could play an active, stabilizing role with your child. Suggest that your ex-husband spend more time with your child. If you're that father, be aware of the important influence you should or could have on your child. Also, remember that the findings in this chapter may not apply to you. They don't necessarily describe everyone. I have friends who are single mothers who have raised sons who don't lie or have any other problems, for that matter.

PEER INFLUENCE: CAN BAD FRIENDS LEAD YOUR CHILD TO LIE?

Jessica is a bright and pretty twelve-year-old girl whose parents are divorced. She lives predominantly with her mother and stepfather, but she spends weekends and school vacations with her single father, who lives half an hour away. Recently she started hanging out with other twelve- and thirteen-year-olds who were clearly below her level of academic achievement but who were among the most popular kids in her class. They were also known to be a rowdy group who defied their parents. Jessica's grades dropped dramatically. She became more independent, often refusing to tell her parents what she planned to do and with whom. She also became interested in boys for the first time. Her mother told her she couldn't date until she was fifteen.

One Saturday afternoon, with her mother's permission, Jessica and two girlfriends met three boys at a local movie theater. As it turned out the boys stood up the girls and Jessica's mother had to pick up the girls. That was how she found out there were only two girls, not three, and that Jessica had lied because she thought her mother would allow a triple date but not a double date. Her parents, upon discovering the lie, were beside themselves. What she lied about wasn't so terrible, but they worried that a bad precedent had been set and their child would start lying about matters of greater concern. *Why couldn't she trust us? Is it our fault? Is it these other kids she's hanging out with? What other lies was she telling? Was this part of a pattern? And how do we get her to stop lying?*

Everyone knows such a story about a child who has "gone wrong" because he or she got in with a bad crowd. It usually involves children approaching puberty or in early adolescence. The research shows that birds of a feather may well flock together. Or, as Hartshorne and May said, "In human affairs, birds that flock together acquire similar plumage."[19]

Most children become more influenced by their friends as they move toward adolescence. They increasingly go along with their friends, even when their friends advocate what their parents consider wrong. The good news is that the situation usually gets better. As young adults, most will become more resistant to peer pressure and won't disregard their parents' views as much.

Hartshorne and May found that children who lie have friends who lie. This association is strongest among friends who are classmates. More recent studies have found that cheaters usually sit adjacent to each other, and that a child who sits near a cheater when taking a school exam is more likely to cheat on the next exam.[20] Kids who are reported to lie the most often have friends who are considered tough or delinquent by the other kids.

Even though all children become more susceptible to peer pressures as they move from childhood through adolescence, not every child will succumb to lying or cheating. An experiment helps to explain why some children become more susceptible to peer pressure and antisocial behavior than others. Psychologists asked children to evaluate their mother, father, adults in general, and kids in terms of their strength, warmth, importance and honesty. They then presented the children with a number of situations. Here's one example:

> You and your friends accidentally find a sheet of paper the teacher must have lost. On this sheet are the questions and answers for tomorrow's quiz. Some of the kids suggest that you say nothing to the teacher about it, so that all of you can get better marks. What would you really do? Suppose your friends decide to go ahead. Would you go along with them or refuse?[21]

Other situations presented to the child included going to a movie recommended by friends but disapproved by parents; not doing homework to be with friends; leaving a sick friend to go to a movie with the gang; joining friends in taking fruit from an orchard marked "no trespassing"; running away after accidentally breaking a window; standing guard while friends put a rubber snake in the teacher's desk; and wearing clothing styles approved by peers but not by parents.

In comparisons of third-, sixth-, eighth-, and eleventh-graders, an ever increasing number said they would go along with their peers in the different misbehaviors. As susceptibility to peer influence increased, favorable evaluations of their fathers usually decreased. But those who maintained favorable views of their fathers and adults in general didn't join with other peers in misbehaviors. (The drawback of this research is that, unlike Hartshorne's and May's study, we are dealing with what children say on a questionnaire, not what they actually did. Fortunately, other research, which compared children's answers to their actions, corroborates this study.[22])

Drs. Edwin Bixenstine, Margaret DeCorte, and Barton Bixenstine, the psychologists who did the research, suggested that their findings show that a "child's growing readiness to affirm peer-sponsored antisocial behavior . . . [is due to] . . . an intense disillusionment with adult veracity, strength, wisdom, importance, good will, and fair-mindedness. The child is not won away from parents to children; rather he is, at least for a time, lost to adults."[23]

They said "for a time" because attitudes toward adults, and in particular toward the father, become more favorable by the eleventh grade. Using some of the same methods, another pair of experiments found similar results and provided more information about the shift back to more favorable attitudes toward parents. In the first experiment, third-, sixth-, ninth- and eleventh-graders were read ten different situations similar to the one I mentioned earlier in which they find the answers to the school exam. Boys conformed, going along with their peers and disregarding their parents' attitudes, more than girls. For both boys and girls those who said they would go along with their peers and participate in misbehavior increased from third to sixth grade, peaked at ninth grade, and decreased among the eleventh-graders.

In the second experiment, the children were given questionnaires to find out how readily they were influenced by their parents. One question asked children to decide whether they should help at the library or teach another child how to swim, while being told their parent advised helping at the library. In another, the children had to decide what to do if their parents asked them to go for a walk when the children wanted to play cards. Conformity to the parent's wishes declined with age.

The relative influence of parents as compared to peers changes as the child develops. Conforming to the parents' wishes was higher than peer conformity in third grade, the youngest group. Most of them sided with parents against peers. By sixth grade it seems as if the children had created two worlds, one for parents and one for friends. Dr. Thomas Berndt, the psychologist who conducted these experiments, said, "Children apparently managed to separate their life in the peer group from their relationship with parents, perhaps by not discussing peers with parents and vice versa."[24]

This is apparently what my son, Tom, did. I asked him why he had secretly given a party when his mother and I were not home, knowing that we and his friends' parents did not allow unchaperoned parties. He said: "You can't understand. I gained so much with my friends. Once it was over I felt bad, I knew I would get caught, but it was worth it."

Dr. Berndt reported that by ninth grade, when peer conformity reaches its peak, there is an actual opposition between parents and peers. There are two reasons why this conflict between parents and peers occurs at this point. First, this is the time when children show the greatest conformity to antisocial behavior. Second, it may be the time in a child's life when the pressure for independence is greatest, as evidenced by studies that show adolescents at this age report the greatest number of disagreements with their parents.

Now the good news. By the end of high school, Dr. Berndt tells us,

> . . . parent-peer relationships entered still another phase. Although some opposition between parent and peer conformity remained, it did not hold for all types of behavior. In addition, peer conformity was decreasing and acceptance of conventional standards for behavior was increasing. The changes suggest an improvement in an adolescent's relationships with parents as the adolescent becomes a young adult.[25]

So far we have been considering the negative influence of friends, but friends can also exert a positive influence. In one study, college students were asked if they would cheat on an exam or lie to the teacher about the reason for their absence. They also had to report whether their friends would approve of their actions. Among those who thought their friends would disapprove, only 27 percent reported cheating or lying, as compared to 78 percent of those who thought their friends would not disapprove.[26] (Though the findings are based on college students, I think they are relevant to adolescents.)

Since bad friends can influence a child in undesirable ways, it's important that you get to know your child's friends. Encourage him or her to invite friends to your home, to play or do homework. Let your child know the friend can stay for dinner or overnight. If your child is spending the night at a friend's house, you should know that friend well enough to know that he or she will not be a negative influence. This may sound like a simple suggestion, but it will save you lots of concern and worry later.

If you know that your child is in with a bad crowd of kids, and you suspect they are engaging in antisocial behavior, be prepared for a real struggle. Attempting to separate your child from those friends will be difficult, no matter what you try. One option is to change schools. Another is to send your child away to spend the summer with relatives. Do anything to get your child out of that group. If that isn't possible, don't give up. Let your child know why you disapprove of lying and antisocial behavior, and that you think spending time with those particular friends encourages that behavior. Hopefully, in time, as your child reaches the end of high school, he or she, like so many other children, will become less influenced by such friends.

DO LIARS COME FROM LESS PRIVILEGED HOMES?

The evidence is contradictory. A number of studies dating back to Hartshorne and May found more lying in lower socioeconomic home environments. However, other studies found no relationship between lying and parents' income. Several studies compared lying among black and white children, but they are inconclusive, as they did not take into account differences in socioeconomic status.

DOES LYING REALLY MATTER?

Some parents may think that is a crazy question. Of course it matters. Lying is wrong, and it is immoral. Other parents may think you shouldn't make a federal case of it. Every kid lies sometimes. We lied when we were kids, and our grandchildren will lie, too. It doesn't really matter. These skeptical parents would change their minds, though, if they thought that a child who lies is likely to grow up to become a criminal. Farfetched? A number of studies have attempted to confirm or negate that theory. Because this is such a pivotal issue for all parents—after all, if lying leads to criminality, then every parent should be concerned—I offer the various sides of the question in detail so you may judge for yourself.

The six such studies I found did not all use the same measures of either lying or later maladjustment. The best of these studies began in 1971, in Buckinghamshire, England. The scientists studied children who were then between five and fifteen years old. One out of every ten students in the public (state) schools was selected at random. Their parents and teachers were sent questionnaires asking about the child's health and behavior. A whopping 93 percent of the parents replied. The scientists learned about the health and behavior patterns of 3,258 boys and roughly the same number of girls. Since very few of the girls got into trouble with the law when they grew up, the scientists focused on the boys.

The questionnaires asked the parents about thirty-seven different types of behavior, including lying, stealing, fussing about food, running away from home, daydreaming, shyness, bad dreams, and destroying property. Two sociologists, Drs. Sheila Mitchell and Peter Rosa, identified the "worst" 10 percent of the boys, described by their parents as having many undesirable traits.[27] The scientists called these boys the "deviators." They compared their criminal records with a "control" group of boys who did not have negative descriptions. They matched the control group boys with the deviators on both age and school. There were 321 boys in each group.

The measure of later criminal behavior was obtained from records of all appearances in court, including juvenile court, for indictable offenses over the next fifteen years. By that time the youngest children would have been twenty and the oldest thirty years old. The offenses considered fall into three categories: theft, damage to property, and interpersonal violence.

The parents' reports about the boys when they were between five and fifteen did predict these subsequent court appearances. What the parents reported about the boys did not predict all crimes, just certain offenses. There were no differences between deviators and controls in fraud, drug offenses, sexual offenses, or drinking offenses. But deviators committed twice as many thefts, property damages, and violent acts than the controls.

Not everything the parent had reported predicted later criminality, only certain traits. In fact, the boys who worried excessively or had food fads had less criminal behavior later. Four childhood traits predicted criminality fifteen years later: stealing, destructiveness, wandering from home, and lying. Let us take a closer look at two of these traits, contrasting lying and stealing.

Instead of comparing the deviators with the controls, let's consider only the deviators. Remember these are the boys who were reported by their parents to have the worst traits. Our questions are: Were there more convictions in later life for those deviators who stole as boys than for those deviators who didn't? Were there more criminal convictions for those in this deviator group who lied as boys than for those who didn't? The answer to both questions is yes.

Seven percent of the boys whose parents said "he never takes anything that belongs to someone else" were convicted for at least one theft within the next fifteen years. Twenty percent of the boys whose parents said their son "has helped himself to someone else's things at least once or twice" had been convicted of a theft. And 61 percent of those boys whose parents said "he has stolen on several occasions" were later convicted of a theft!

The predictions about lying were not as strong, but the relationship is there. Four percent of the boys whose parents said they "always tell the truth" were later convicted of a theft. Twelve percent of the boys whose parents said "he tells an occasional fib" were convicted of a theft. And 36 percent of the boys whose parents said "he tells deliberate untruths quite often" were convicted of a theft within the next fifteen years.

The teachers' descriptions also predicted later criminality, especially multiple convictions. Of those boys that the teacher had said often tell lies, the percent who appeared in court more than once was six times higher than it was for more truthful boys. The figure is identical for those the teacher had said stole.*

There are a number of cautions we should bear in mind before becoming too alarmed. Look at those figures again. Almost two thirds, 64 percent, of those boys who, according to their parents, lied as children did not become criminals as adults. At the same time, it is astounding that one third of those who were reported to lie had criminal offenses so many years later.

Some crucial information is missing. Is a lie by a five- or six-year-old as good a predictor as a lie by a ten- or fifteen-year-old? How many years were there between the reports of frequent lying and first court appearances? Does this depend on the age of the child when lying was first reported? We also need to know whether the combination of both lying and stealing is worse than either one alone. Unfortunately, the answers to these questions are not available, because the study was done some years ago and to protect confidentiality the records were destroyed. The

---

*When the ratings of both teachers and parents are combined, the prediction was better, but the numbers were very small. There were only fourteen children identified by both parents and teachers as lying often. Half of them were later convicted of a theft. There were only seven children identified by both parents and teachers as stealing, and four of them were later convicted of a theft. Although suggestive, the number of cases is too small to give the results much emphasis.

authors of the study remember that only lies in later childhood predict trouble as an adult. Also, both stealing and lying led to later trouble more than lying alone.

Clearly the evidence suggests that for a sizable number of boys lying as a child foretells antisocial criminal behavior as an adult. This study suggests that lying may be a warning sign, but I have to emphasize—may be. Most of the boys who lied or stole did not become criminals, and we don't know why most didn't while some did. Were they different kinds of lies? Did the parents respond to the lies differently? Did the boys who became criminals lie about different things? Did something else happen in their life that set some of these boys back onto the right track? Are the kids who become criminals the same ones who continued lying throughout their childhood, while the others abandoned lying? Were the liars who became criminals the lousiest liars, those who weren't very clever, and who therefore got caught when they became adults? Did the children who didn't become criminals have parents who were overly sensitive to lying, and exaggerated how much their children had lied? There are no answers to these questions. The research has not been done.

The crucial question is: What role does lying play in a child's development of antisocial behavior? Is lying a symptom of a more serious problem or is it a cause of subsequent problems? Is lying just part of what kids who get into trouble do? If a smart-aleck kid throws a spitball when the teacher's back is turned, that kid will probably deny it even when asked point-blank. By this reasoning, children who are getting into trouble will lie, but not every child who lies will get into trouble.

The contrary view is that lying is itself a step, perhaps a pivotal step, in leading the child into a pattern of antisocial behavior. Lying may be one of the earliest signs that a child is headed in a bad direction. Dodging responsibility, learning you can get away with things, sneaking to succeed, may teach the child to break other rules. Lying may be the first sign that trouble is brewing. If a child gets away with lying, this might lead the child to take the risks involved in other antisocial acts.

No one yet knows. The research needed has not yet begun. There is no "correct view." Perhaps both are correct, depending on the child. And perhaps the answer differs depending upon how old the child is when he or she starts to lie frequently, and how long that pattern is maintained.

In my opinion, the evidence is sufficient to say that if your child's frequent lying persists, take it seriously. But let me also add that while you should take it seriously, remember that the majority of boys who lie at an early age do *not get into trouble with the law in later life.*

OVERVIEW

There is no clear-cut, simple, or decisive answer as to why some kids lie more than others. If the child has the talent to succeed on a test without lying, he or she probably won't. The child who is smart enough to recognize the risks of being caught isn't likely to lie. But when the risk is low, or intelligence is not the talent required to obtain a goal, then being smart does not preclude lying.

Kids who lie a lot are more maladjusted than those who don't, and lying as a child does predict a greater chance of later trouble with the law. But most kids who lie don't get into trouble later in life, and we don't know if lying is a symptom or a cause of maladjustment.

There is some evidence that lying is part of a more general personality pattern, most often and most ably performed by children who manipulate others to their own ends. This manipulative pattern is evident in some children by the age of ten. No one has found out how much earlier it may appear, nor has anyone resolved exactly the role the parents play in the development of this pattern.

Some kids—but not all—who lack parental supervision lie more often. Children are influenced to lie by friends who lie or engage in antisocial behavior that they lie about to avoid getting punished. Peer pressure, as we all know, is strongest in adolescence. Interestingly, how the boy feels about his father plays a role. The adolescent boys who respected their father were less susceptible to peer pressure. And, we can say with a sigh of relief, most kids lie less when they pass through the initial phases of adolescence.

Whether or not a child will lie in a particular situation depends not just on the factors we have considered but also on the nature of each specific situation. It is not just the characteristics of the child, nor just the influence of the child's family and friends that matters. Whether a child will lie depends also on what is at stake. The influence of the specific temptation probably matters more at an earlier than a later age. In the words of Drs. Hartshorne and May: "Honesty appears to be a congeries of specialized acts which are closely tied up with particular features of the situation in which deception is a possibility. . . . Motives for cheating, lying, and stealing are highly complex, and are specialized just as are the acts of deception.[28]

Which factors are most important—intelligence, personality, maladjustment, parenting, friends, the specifics of the situation? No one knows, for the type of research that would allow an answer to that question has not yet been done. My bet is that the relative importance of these factors would differ depending upon age (obviously so for the influence of friends) and individual characteristics of each child.

CHAPTER THREE

Lying at Different Ages

HOW EARLY CAN CHILDREN LIE?

Lori is an energetic three-and-a-half-year-old with an artistic spirit. One day she decided to express her creativity on her bedroom wall with her new crayons. To her it was a great work of art. To her mother, however, it was not a pretty picture.

"Lori, did you draw on your wall?" her mother asked, obviously upset.

"No," Lori answered, completely straight-faced.

"Well, who did it?"

"It wasn't me, Mommy," she replied, still the innocent angel.

"Was it a little ghost?" her mother asked sarcastically.

"Yeah, yeah," Lori said. "It was a ghost." She stuck to her story until her mother finally said, "Well, you better tell that little ghost not to do it again or she'll be sorry."

Some people think young children are too innocent to lie. Others think they would if they could but they lack ability. The evidence suggests that kids are capable of lying at an earlier age than most adults give them credit for.

By four years of age, and perhaps earlier, some children can and will lie. They are not simply making mistakes, or confusing fantasy with reality, but deliberately attempting to mislead.

Lies at this age are not a terrible problem. All children, and most adults, lie sometimes. However, parents should start to worry when a child lies frequently, especially if the lying persists for a long period. When lying first appears, parents should discuss with their child the moral issues involved. As we will see, children's understanding of these issues changes enormously from the age of four to fourteen.

Several studies suggest that children can lie at a much earlier age than thought by adults unfamiliar with childhood behavior. In one, Dr. Stephen Ceci and one of his students tempted preschool children to lie to protect someone they liked from punishment.[1] Children were left in a room with a toy that they were told not to play with. When the experimenter left the room, an adult played with the forbidden toy and broke it. When the adult left the room, the investigator returned and asked the child what happened. Children were divided into two groups: those who already knew and liked the adult (a "mentor" with whom they had formed a bond) and those to whom the adult was a stranger. Almost half of the children did not inform on the mentor. Some said they didn't know who broke the toy, others said someone else broke it. All of the three-and-a-half- to four-year-olds, however, told the truth and informed on the adult stranger.

In another study,[2] three-year-old boys and girls were taken into a room, seated facing away from a table, and told that the experimenter was going to put a surprise toy on the table and leave. The child was asked not to peek, and was told he or she could play with the toy when the experimenter came back to the room. The experimenter then left, while the child's mother filled out a questionnaire sitting with her back to the child. After the child either peeked or when five minutes had gone by, the experimenter came back and asked the child, "Did you peek?"

Twenty-nine out of the thirty-three children peeked. When asked if they had peeked, there was nearly a three-way split among those who confessed, those who denied peeking, and those who gave no response at all. The boys were more forthcoming than the girls (two thirds of the boys admitted peeking, only 15 percent of the girls admitted it).

In still another study[3] mothers and teachers of four-year-old children were asked if children of different ages would deliberately tell a lie. The percent who reported that children lied increased with the age of the child. Here are the findings:

Age	Percent of Parents and Teachers Who Said Children of This Age Lie
3	33
4	75
5	90
6	100

Together these three studies show that at least some children as young as three or four will deliberately lie. Of course, the negative consequences for lying were not high in either of the experiments. If the investigator had emphasized beforehand to the children the importance of being truthful, or the costs of lying, fewer would have lied. The issue addressed by these experiments was not *when* children lie, but whether children of such young ages can lie under any conditions. Until this work, most scientists believed that three- to six-year-olds were not considered able to distinguish between unintentionally making a mistake and deliberately saying something true.[4]

HOW EARLY DO CHILDREN UNDERSTAND THE CONCEPT OF LYING?

How well can they lie? Is it easier to spot their lie than the lie of an older child? Are they more swayed by suggestion than older children, more influenced by how questions are asked and the beliefs of adults? Are four-year-olds more likely to be "auto-suggestible" than older children? That is, are they likely to start believing their lies the more often they tell them?

In order to answer those questions, let's examine how children think about lying.

Keith, a six-year-old boy, divides his time between his father's house and his mother's. One time Keith's father planned to pick him up at noon so the two could go to a baseball game. But Keith's father didn't know his mother had already had a tennis lesson arranged at the same time. When Keith found out that he wouldn't be going to the game with his father, he called his dad, hurt and angry.

"You lied," Keith cried. "Why did you lie?" His father sympathized and tried to explain he hadn't lied, it was just a scheduling misunderstanding. But Keith would have none of it. All he knew was his father had said they were going to a ball game—and they weren't.

Up until about eight years of age, children consider any false statement a lie, regardless of whether the person who said it knew it was false. Intention is not the issue—only whether information is false or true. Even when young children know the speaker does not intend to mislead, they still call him a liar if he unwittingly provides false information. But the majority of eight-year-olds, as with adults, do not consider a person a liar if they know that person is giving false information unwittingly.

It would be easy to explain the young children's definition of lying as reflecting their inability to deal with subtle matters such as intent. Outcome is all that matters in the undeveloped moral thinking of such young children, according to some writers. A remarkable series of recent studies in Austria by Drs. Wimmer, Gruber, and Perner[5] found this is not so. The very same children who don't recognize the import of intent in their definition of lying do respond to intent when it comes to their moral judgment of the person making the false statement. In their study they read and acted out with dolls the following story:

> Mother returns from her shopping trip. She bought chocolate for a cake. Maxi may help her put away the things. He asks her: "Where should I put the chocolate?" "In the blue cupboard," says the mother. Maxi puts the chocolate into the blue cupboard. Maxi remembers exactly where he put the chocolate so that he could come back and get some later. He loves chocolate. Then he leaves for the playground. Mother starts preparing the cake and takes the chocolate out of the

blue cupboard. She grates a bit into the dough and then she does not put it back into the blue cupboard but into the green one. Maxi is not present. He doesn't know that the chocolate is now in the green cupboard. After a while Maxi returns from the playground, hungry, and he wants to get some chocolate. He still remembers where he had put the chocolate. However, before Maxi gets to look for the chocolate his sister comes into the kitchen. She says to Maxi: "I heard that Mother has bought some chocolate. I would like to have some now; do you know where the chocolate is?"

Four different versions of this story were read to young children. In one version Maxi wants to be truthful, but he gives her false information (tells her it is in the blue cupboard) because he doesn't know Mother transferred it. In the second version the line about Mother transferring the chocolate from the blue to the green cupboard is left out of the story, so when Maxi wants to be truthful and says it is in the blue cupboard, he is actually giving correct information. In the next two stories the children are told that Maxi wants to deceive his sister. The following lines are added to the stories: " 'Good grief,' thinks Maxi, 'now my sister wants to eat all the chocolate. But I want to keep it all to myself. I must tell her something completely wrong so that she won't find it.' " If the line about Mom transferring the chocolate from the blue to the green cupboard is left in, then we have a story in which Maxi wants to mislead but he unwittingly tells the truth. And if the line about the cupboard transfer is left out, Maxi wants to mislead and does pass on false information about the location of the chocolate. The chart below shows the four conditions in the experiment.

	Story 1	Story 2	Story 3	Story 4
Where Maxi thinks chocolate is	Blue cabinet	Blue cabinet	Blue cabinet	Blue cabinet
Where chocolate is	Green cabinet	Green cabinet	Green cabinet	Green cabinet
Maxi's intent	Truthful	Truthful	Misleading	Misleading
Maxi's effect	Wrong information	Correct information	Correct information	Wrong information

The majority of the four- and six-year-old boys and girls said Maxi was lying not only when he intended to lie and did give false information (story 4), but also when Maxi wanted to be truthful and share with his sister but misled her because he didn't know that Mother had transferred the location of the chocolate (story 1). Intent didn't matter. But intent did matter to these children when they were asked whether they would give Maxi a golden star because he was nice to his sister or a black point because he was nasty to her. The majority of the children (75 percent) based their moral judgment on Maxi's intent.*

Even though these young children misused the term "lying," they did understand intentionality. They knew that it was bad to intend to mislead someone. Although this may seem obvious to some readers, until just a few years ago, when this study was reported, the scientific literature maintained that such young children did not make moral judgments based on intent.

If they do make moral judgments based on intent, one might ask why young children do not use intent in their definition of lying. Some of the earliest researchers[6] on lying in children (1909) suggested the reason may be because parents don't adequately explain lying. Parents stress that children should tell the truth, without explaining that to say something false is not a lie if you don't know it's false. Other research suggests that it may have more to do with developing language skills.

What's important is that children as young as four, and perhaps earlier, do know that intending to mislead someone is bad. Such very young children condemn lying more than older children or adults. In the words of one researcher, young children are "fanatics of truth."[7] Certainly, younger children think it is more wrong to lie than do older children. For example, 92 percent of five-year-olds said it is always wrong to lie. By age eleven that figure had shrunk to only 28 percent.

---

*Developmental psychologists who work in Piaget's tradition might discount this finding by supposing that the children judged the lies as bad only because there were negative consequences. Importantly, this study included features that made it possible to determine that was not so, and the findings can be interpreted as I have.

Paralleling that change, 75 percent of the five-year-olds said they never lied, while none of the eleven-year-olds made such a claim to virtue.[8]

Drs. Candida Peterson, James Peterson and Diane Seeto who obtained this information also asked children about whether different types of lies are wrong. All age groups, from five through eleven, said that lies to avoid punishment (e.g., not admitting you spilled ink on the bedspread) are worse than white lies (e.g., telling another child you like his haircut even though you don't). Altruistic lies (e.g., not telling a bully who wants to beat up a younger child where the child is when you know) were not condemned by most age groups. The five-year-olds gave even this lie a lower rating than the older children, although even they thought it was not as bad as the lie to avoid being punished.

These investigators also asked the children what happens when lies are told. The five- to nine-year-old children mentioned punishment most often. At this young age, punishment is the deterrent. Less than a third of the eleven-year-olds mentioned punishment, while half of them said that lying destroys trust, a consequence mentioned by few of the younger kids.

Marie Vasek found similar results in interviews with boys and girls from ages six through twelve.[9] She read the children such stories as the following:

Bob and some of his friends were having a snowball fight in Bob's front yard. After a while, they got tired of throwing snowballs at each other and decided to throw snowballs at passing cars. They were all throwing snowballs but one of Bob's hit a car's windshield. The driver stopped the car and got out. All the kids took off for their homes. The driver had seen Bob throw the snowball and run into the house, so he went up and knocked on Bob's front door. Bob's mom came up from the basement to answer the door. She had not seen what the kids were doing, but the driver told her what had happened. She went and found Bob and he said that they were only having a snowball fight. He had thrown a snowball at a friend and the other guy ducked and the snowball hit the car accidentally. Everybody ran because they didn't want to get in trouble.[10]

According to Vasek, the youngest children said that the main reason anyone lies is to avoid punishment, as in this story. While they thought it was wrong to lie, they understood why people did it. Young children of five and six, she concluded, will lie to "... avoid punishment whenever they suspect that they have done something for which they should be punished. ... [It is] a choice for the child between telling the truth and taking one's chances [of being punished] or telling another lie to avoid punishment for the first."[11]

By age ten to twelve, and perhaps earlier, children no longer consider lying always wrong; they become more "flexible." Whether a lie is wrong depends on the outcome of the situation. For example, in my interviews with children, a twelve-year-old named Bessie said, "What if someone asked you if their hair looks nice and it didn't. You would want to lie." An eleven-year-old boy, Robert, told me the following story when I asked him to give me an example of when lying is okay: "Say some kid is a real bad guy, a bully or something, who hurts other kids. Then if you lied and said he did it, even if he didn't, he would get in trouble, and since he hurts people it's okay if he gets punished."

While preadolescents or early adolescents understand the idea that lying is wrong because people will no longer trust you, that is not always foremost in their minds. Even adults don't always remember the consequence of losing trust when they consider whether to lie. Relationships may not be the same once a lie has violated trust. The loss of trust is difficult to repair; sometimes it is never reparable.

In an article appearing in 1987 in *The Washington Post Magazine*, writer Walt Harrington described how even a white lie, once discovered, changed how friends feel about each other. The writer, a male, has lunch with a woman friend who has recently had an affair with a male friend of his. "She didn't tell her husband about the affair, which is lie no. 1. The man she had the affair with swore to her that he didn't tell me, which is lie no. 2. And as we sit eating lunch, she is about to maneuver me into lie no. 3 by unexpectedly telling the truth: 'I had an affair. Do you know about it?' " The writer decides not to break his promise to her lover and denies it. A few days later he told her that he had been lying when he denied knowing about the affair. " 'You're a very good liar,' she said. 'I believed you.' " He asks if she is angry with him. " 'No,' she said slowly, 'not angry. But it does change the way I think of you. Not a lot, but it does change the way I think of you.' "[12]

Loss of trust is the point I emphasize in my conversations about lying with my own children. I explain how difficult life together would be if we couldn't trust each other not to lie. I also explain how hard it is to trust someone again once that trust has been violated. Once you know your child has made the choice to lie, doubts and suspicions may not be so easily dismissed. It is not an easy lesson for them to learn. It is not an easy lesson for anyone to learn. Only those who have been caught in a lie and lost the trust of someone close understand the implications.

Some child psychologists believe that you can teach children these ideas by telling them stories. The story "The Boy Who Cried Wolf" is such an example. As you may recall, the story recounts how a young boy falsely claimed he was being attacked by a wolf so many times that when he actually was being attacked by a wolf no one believed him. I remember being very impressed by the moral lesson of that tale when I was five or six. I don't remember ever thinking about it when I lied to my parents or to my friends when I was an adolescent. Perhaps if my parents had continued instilling moral values as I grew older, it would have stuck with me. I learned through experience in late adolescence, in two unhappy romantic relationships, how hard it is to reestablish trust once you have been betrayed.

DOES THE FREQUENCY OF LYING CHANGE WITH AGE?

A number of studies have asked this question, and the findings are divided. Some studies find no change, while some have found a decrease in lying among older children. In either case, at every age only a minority of the children are reported to lie. Perhaps most interesting is the finding that from early childhood through late adolescence the percentage of children who lie *often* remains about the same. It is a low figure, less than 5 percent.[13] From what we learned in the last chapter, these are the children who are most likely to be at risk for developing other difficulties in their lives.

Two problems in this research merit mention. First, since the data comes from the reports of parents and teachers, we must remember that they may not be a completely accurate source because of the halo/horns effect discussed earlier. As we will see, children do become more successful liars as they grow older. Conceivably, children might lie more as they grow older, but because their lies are less detectable, their parents and teachers might say they lied the same amount or less.

The other problem is how to interpret the finding that the percentage of frequent liars remains about the same. There are two possibilities about who these chronic liars are.[14] One possibility is that these liars who show up early in life, perhaps at five or six, remain chronic liars throughout childhood and adolescence. The other possibility is that being a chronic liar is a transitory phase a few kids go through. By this reasoning, the kids who show up as chronic liars at age seven would not be the same ones as those found at age eleven. The only way to find out which possibility is true is to follow the same children for many years. That kind of longitudinal study has not been done. All we have are cross-sectional studies of different children in each age group.

What's most likely is that both possibilities occur. For some kids, chronic lying is a phase, and due to either parental intervention or reduced pressures, the chronic lying stops. Others may continue on what may become a fixed pattern for dealing with the world.

If your child shows evidence of being a chronic liar, you won't know whether it is a phase or the beginning of what could be a lifelong path. Chronic lying should be taken seriously; don't wait to find out if it's a phase. Try to find out why your child is lying. Examine your own behavior. Are you doing something that in some way encourages or forces your child to lie? Is your child lying in response to some other problem at home? Is it due to the influence of friends, as I suggested earlier? In any case, explain to your child why lying is harmful. If you don't think you are succeeding, then seek counseling.

DO KIDS GET BETTER AT LYING AS THEY GROW UP?

Young children believe adults are all powerful. A five-year-old, in her own imaginative way, explained, "You should never tell a lie because the brains inside grownups' heads are so smart they find out!"[15]

However, children find out earlier than most parents think that they can get away with their lies at least some of the time. By early adolescence, and perhaps even earlier, by ten or eleven, most children become fairly able liars. No longer are they always betrayed by the sound of their voice, the look on their face, blatant inconsistencies in what they say, or outlandish alibis. As children gain the power to mislead, parents lose the certainty they had earlier. Although they may still catch a lie—older children, like adults, do sometimes make some mistakes when they lie, and many lies are betrayed by an accidental discovery—parents learn that they no longer know what their kids are thinking, feeling, doing, or planning, unless their children want them to know.

Two thirds of the first-graders we asked said their parents could tell when they were lying, while less than half of the seventh-graders said their parents could tell. Consistent with that, most eleventh-graders said they were in fifth or sixth grade when they first were able to lie without being caught.

There is no long-nosed Pinocchio sign of lying in children or adults, no muscle twitch, no voice inflection, no body movement that is a clear-cut sign of lying—no indication that a person is lying or telling the truth. Yet there are behavioral clues to deceit. Sometimes the clue is contained in what the person says. The account is too farfetched, inconsistent, or directly contradicts the facts. Often the clue that someone is lying is not in what is said but how it is said. The sound of the voice, the look on the face, the movement of a hand may not fit the words. The liar may look guilty or sound fearful, or seem too excited to be credible.

As they become older, children not only become more skilled in telling lies to others, they also become more skilled in detecting when they are being lied to.[16] Mom's false excuse for why she couldn't make it to the school play, Dad's claim he wasn't shouting angrily, he just wanted to be heard over the TV—these will no longer always be believed. It's not that children become so good at catching lies; it is rather that they start out so bad at it that any improvement appears significant. My own research and that of many others has shown that most people are fooled most of the time by lies.[17] The improvement that comes with age is more in the ability to tell a lie, not so much the ability to tell when someone else is lying. I found only six scientific studies that attempt to discover if children become more successful liars as they grow up. The results provide some support for what every teenager's parent already knows: older kids *are* better liars than younger kids. Since kids improve at everything as they develop, these studies are not very instructive.

One reason such a study may not provide conclusive findings is that a comparison of age groups should be based on the same lie. That in itself is not easy, for the same reasons that a six-year-old and a sixteen-year-old don't play with the same games or watch the same TV programs. The lie has to be understandable, be interesting, and seem reasonable across the entire age span studied. The children at each age have to be similarly motivated to succeed in telling the lie. And the scientist has to worry about the ethics of asking children to lie, careful not to teach them lying techniques unwittingly or that lying may be a good thing to do.

In two studies the children were asked to lie about how they liked the taste of grape juice. In one of the experiments, five- to twelve-year-old children, along with some college students, were given two drinks. One was a sweetened grape beverage, the other was made without sugar. The children were told to convince a twenty-four-year-old woman interviewer that the drinks tasted good, no matter how they actually tasted. In the second study, some of the children were also asked to lie by saying they disliked the sweet drink. Drs. Robert Feldman, Larry Jenkins, and Oladeji Popoola told the children "that the point of the experiment was to determine how much ability . . . [they] . . . had in deceiving the interviewer. Television commercials that were well known to the subject were mentioned to illustrate the kind of responses desired."[18]

Another study showed unpleasant and pleasant slides to first- and fifth-graders. On half of the slides the children were asked to lie by showing an emotion opposite to what they felt. On some of the unpleasant slides they were asked to look as if they had pleasant feelings, and on some of the pleasant slides to look as if they had unpleasant feelings.[19] In still another study, boys and girls from six to twelve years of age were asked to pretend they were actors being interviewed about their likes and dislikes. They were told to show how well they could act by pretending to like or be neutral about something they actually disliked, and by pretending to dislike or be neutral about something they liked.[20]

The one consistent finding across all the studies is that children in the first grade (five and six years old) are less successful liars—that is, more *detectable*—than children ten and older. Less clear was whether girls were better liars than boys, or whether the lies were less detectable if a positive or negative feeling was being concealed.

WHY SOME LIES ARE HARD TO TELL

When emotions are not involved, it is easier to lie—easier to lie about facts, plans, actions, or ideas than about not being angry, afraid, or feeling any other emotion. It is much easier to lie about not being angry yesterday than to conceal anger felt at the moment. It is easier to conceal mild irritation than fury. Even when the lie is not about emotions, the emotions involved with lying—fear of being caught, guilt about lying, or the challenge and excitement of putting one over (I call it "duping delight")—can make it harder to lie successfully.

A parent told me about an incident that illustrates how it's easier to lie when there is some distance from emotions. The subject of dentists usually brings up strong emotions—usually fear—in both children and adults. Aaron, a thirteen-year-old boy who had been having trouble with his teeth, was asked by his uncle if he had been to the dentist lately.

"Yeah," Aaron replied. "I went last week."

"So how was it?" his uncle inquired. "Did it hurt?"

"No, not a bit. It was a piece of cake," Aaron said without a moment's hesitation. Later the uncle found out the boy hadn't been to the dentist in several months, and when he did go, he had been very fearful about the Novocain injections.

Several months later the uncle again inquired whether Aaron had been to the dentist. This time the uncle noticed that the boy looked away, didn't say anything for a moment, quickly replied no, then just as quickly proceeded into a long review of a movie he had seen the night before. As it turned out, Aaron had been to the dentist just the previous week, and from his parents' report, had had two wisdom teeth pulled and had complained and cried a lot.

Emotions, particularly when they are strong, produce involuntary changes in behavior that are difficult to conceal. These changes may be registered anywhere or everywhere—in the face, hand movements, posture, or the sound of the voice. To succeed, the liar must suppress all of those emotion signs that don't fit the lie. The liar must be able to monitor and control his or her behavior. That is not easy for most adults; it is even harder for young children. Strong emotions and the effort expended to control signs of those emotions can also be distracting to such a degree that it is hard for the liar to think straight and talk convincingly.

GUILT ABOUT LYING

In the experiments examining whether older kids are better at lying than younger kids, an important factor was eliminated: guilt. The kids were told to lie; the scientists *authorized* lying, and a plausible reason (being on a TV show) was given as the rationale. When a child forges a better grade on his report card, or claims not to have drunk the Scotch in the liquor cabinet, no one in authority tells the child to lie. That's the child's choice, made against the wishes of the parents or teacher. It is then, when lying is not requested or authorized, that the child may feel guilt. These feelings of guilt make it harder to lie. They are a burden on the liar, and may cause the lie to fail.

Guilt may eventually cause the liar to confess, such is its weight and pain. Relieving that weight often motivates a confession. Tim, a ten-year-old, put it this way: "I don't know, it's like sometimes if you told a bad lie, it'd be on your conscience and you have to tell somebody. If it's something really bad. Just to get it out of ya and it won't bug you any more."[21] Even if the liar tries to maintain the lie, the signs of guilt—the averted gaze, flattened or agitated sound of the voice—may betray the liar's pretense.

Not all children, of course, feel guilty when they lie. At younger ages most children believe lying is always wrong. By adolescence most kids are no longer convinced that all lies are bad. Parents I have interviewed said that if you raise your child correctly, your child will feel guilt if he or she lies to you. There is no research that I know of to support that hope. My research on adults suggests that people don't feel guilt about lying to a target they don't respect, with whom they don't share values. I expect that children are less likely to feel guilty about lying to parents who impose what they think are unjust, harsh, and inflexible rules, just as adults don't feel guilt about lying to an employer they think has been unfair to them. Guilt about lying is strongest when the liar shares values with the victim of the lie.

Rachel is a sophomore in high school and takes great pride in her academic achievement. Her parents, both college professors, are also proud of her and have always stressed the importance of getting good grades. When she did poorly on an end-of-the-week science quiz for which she hadn't prepared, she lied to her parents, saying that she had done well. But over the weekend her parents noticed she acted sullen and listless, very much unlike herself. When guests came and Rachel's parents bragged about her school achievement, she brusquely left the room. Sunday evening Rachel could not hold it in any longer and admitted her lie to her parents.

A child can easily justify lying to the parent who seems to be indulging in actions forbidden to the child. If you get drunk, for instance, your adolescent may think it hypocritical that you punish him or her for becoming intoxicated. Many adults don't feel guilty about lying to anonymous targets, or institutions like Ma Bell or Uncle Sam. That's probably why I have never convinced my son, Tom, that it is wrong to lie about his age when seeking a child's discount at a movie theater or on public transportation. He knows many adults cheat and doesn't understand why we don't. Further, he doesn't understand why we expect him to live according to standards that others he knows don't follow.

There may not be guilt about lying when the liar believes that everyone else is lying. That's what some preadolescents claim. Although there is no scientific evidence to support it, I suspect this is one reason why adolescents are more successful liars. They feel less guilt about lying to their parents or teachers. Rejecting parental values, one form of rebellion, noticing clay feet that authority stands upon, is common in many adolescents. For some, lying may be one way of establishing their own identity, of separating, and achieving independence—a necessary stage of adolescence.

Few people, children or adults, feel guilty about trivial lies. When the liar believes the lie won't hurt anyone, not even the target of the lie, guilt is relatively absent. Even when the lie is of great consequence, liars don't feel guilty when lying is authorized. Spies feel no guilt about their deceit because lying has been authorized by the country for which they are working.

If someone in authority tells the child to lie, there is little likelihood the child will feel any guilt about the act. Lying is easier without guilt. In all the experiments I have described (except for Hartshorne and May, and the experiments I described in the beginning of this chapter), since the lies were authorized by the scientists, the children's lies were relatively guilt free. Therefore they do not reveal much about most of the lies children tell to their parents or teachers.

FEAR OF BEING CAUGHT

I suspect that the children in the experiments on lying had no reason to fear the consequences of being caught, no reason to think that if they failed to be convincing they would lose anything or be punished. However, most of the lies between parents or teachers and children have negative consequences if discovered. In lies that matter, the liar is afraid of being caught because of the likelihood of being punished.

This is one way to differentiate between trivial and important lies: Would the liar be punished if caught lying? What is the price of being caught? Often there are two punishments—one for lying itself, the other for the act the lie was designed to conceal.

Like guilt, fear of being caught makes lying harder, may motivate a confession, and can produce signs in face, body, and voice that betray the lie. That fear can become a torment, and people may confess in order to obtain relief from it. Fear can disorganize the liar's attempts to maintain a consistent line. It can generate changes in how the liar talks, in the sound of the voice, in the expression on the face, which contradict what the liar is saying and ultimately betray the lie.

Ten-year-old Charlotte, who is something of a tomboy, loved the new Guess jeans her mother bought her. Her mother warned her that they were expensive and Charlotte should take care not to ruin them. She wore them to school almost every day. One day while sliding into second base playing baseball, she badly ripped one leg of the jeans. She rushed home, and before her mother could see her, Charlotte hid the jeans in the bottom of her drawer. A week later Charlotte's mother suggested she wear the jeans with a new blouse. Charlotte stammered and said she would rather wear a skirt, which is not typical of Charlotte. Her mother was suspicious. When she asked to see the jeans, Charlotte said she left them at her friend Karen's—except Charlotte had not been to Karen's house in over a week.

Not everyone who lies is afraid of being caught. That fear is usually strongest when the stakes are high, when the consequences of being caught are great. Even then, some liars are more vulnerable to fear. The target's reputation also influences how much fear the liar feels. Young children who believe their parents' omnipotent claim that they can always spot a lie will be more afraid of being caught than older kids who have learned that they can sometimes get away with it.

In almost all research on deception in adults or children, scientists have studied white lies or trivial lies in which not much is at stake, rather than important ones. In unauthorized lies, trust is at stake, and no one wants to be distrusted. The experiments we've been looking at did not risk trust because the kids would probably never again see the people against whom they lied.

DUPING DELIGHT

There is a third set of feelings that can betray a lie. I call it "duping delight." It includes the excitement of fooling someone, meeting the challenge of "putting one over on someone." There may be a sense of accomplishment and exhilaration, a feeling of power and achievement. It may be felt by an adult deceiving a spouse, or a child misleading a parent. I suspect that in adolescence this challenge and exercise of power can be an important factor motivating the decision to lie. Even at younger ages children may think of lying as a kind of enjoyable game. In fact, many games for both children and adults involve lying. Poker is a perfect example. So is a game children play called "Who Has the Button." Playing such games develops and exercises the skills involved in lying.[22]

Duping delight, in its own way, can motivate a confession when the liar wants to win someone's admiration. Criminals often are caught because they can't resist boasting about how clever they were in a particular scam. Children may be tempted to share their accomplishment by telling a buddy how easily they misled Mom or Dad. A child is less likely to feel duping delight when lying to a parent, more often when putting one over on a gullible friend, particularly if some buddies are around to enjoy the performance.

Stephanie and Jason, two fourth-graders, liked to tease other kids, particularly Steven, the "new kid." One time during recess in the school-yard, Stephanie and Jason had convinced Steven they were brother and sister. They explained that their parents were divorced and that when they split up the daughter went to live with the mom and the son moved in with the father. As they elaborated, a group of other kids (who knew Stephanie and Jason weren't related) gathered around to enjoy the show. When Jason embellished the tale by adding that his father was remarried—to the school principal—the pair couldn't hold back their giggles, and they broke out laughing.

PREPARING THE LINE

Lies fail not only because emotional signs—guilt, fear, and duping delight—betray the liar. They also fail when the liar doesn't prepare ahead of time.

Lies are easier when the liar knows beforehand exactly when he or she will need to lie. That advance notice allows the liar time to invent a credible false line and rehearse it, time to anticipate questions and devise answers. Suppose a girl intends to go out with a boyfriend her parents have said she cannot see. To make sure she is not caught, she needs time to work up a cover story—like spending the night at her girlfriend's house—and to anticipate the questions that might be asked the next day. She needs a reasonable-sounding explanation when her dad says he tried to reach her but there was no answer at her friend's house. When people have to make up an answer on the spot, there are often telltale clues. Pauses will increase. They may look away. The voice may become less animated. These are not signs of lying itself; they are signs of on-the-spot thinking. If you ask your teenager, "Do you think Gorbachev will stay in power?" you would expect to see signs of thinking, since most kids have not thought about that question. But if the question is "Where were you last night when I phoned Sally's home? No one answered," then the signs of thinking about her reply probably would indicate lying, since she should not need time to think—that is, if she is telling the truth.

Practice makes a perfect liar. The more often you tell a lie, the better you tell it. Partly that's because you learn that you can get away with it, and your budding confidence deflates any fear of being caught. If a child has learned that Mom is a pushover for a certain type of lie, there is less fear of being caught. Repeated lying also decreases the chance of feeling guilt about the lie. The question of whether lying is right or wrong usually comes up the first time one contemplates telling a lie. That's when guilt can interfere with the success of a lie. But after the first time, lying becomes easier with each successive time. By the second or third time the same lie has been told, less consideration is given to moral ramifications or possible negative consequences. Lawyers refer to this pattern of sliding into more and more illegal acts as the "slippery slope."

Sometimes people actually start to believe their lie if they tell it often enough. The kid who boosts his reputation by the story he fabricates about staring down the tough guy may forget it didn't really happen after the third or fourth telling, like the fisherman who truly begins to buy his own tall tale about "the huge fish that got away." The fisherman or the boastful child, if challenged, can remember the actual facts, but it may take some effort. This ability to deceive even oneself has a side benefit for the aspiring liar: When people believe their own lie, they make fewer mistakes when they lie. In a sense—at least in their own minds—they are telling the truth. Although I know of no research on this, I expect that very young children are more susceptible to this effect.

The following chart summarizes the variables that make lying easy or difficult:

	Hard to Lie	Easy to Lie
The stakes are:	High	Low
Punished if caught for lying:	Yes	No
Punished if caught for act the lie conceals:	Yes	No
Experience getting away with this lie:	No	Yes
Target of lie is gullible:	No	Yes
Respect for target of lie:	Yes	No
Share values with target of lie:	Yes	No
Lie is authorized:	No	Yes
Target is harsh, unfair, unjust:	No	Yes
Challenge to mislead target:	Yes	No
Others knowingly witness the deceit:	Yes	No
Can anticipate when need to lie:	No	Yes

DEVELOPING THE ABILITIES TO LIE

Many of the abilities that develop with age—abilities necessary for children to take increasing responsibility for themselves—also allow them to be more successful if they choose to lie. Abraham Lincoln is reputed to have said that he didn't have a good enough memory to lie. But not all lies require a good memory. Lies in which nothing false is said—I call them concealment lies—do not depend on memory. Here's a typical concealment lie in which a good memory is not necessary: When Mom asks how his day was, Johnny doesn't mention he was kept after school by the principal, who threatens that the next time Johnny throws a spitball at the teacher he will be suspended. Johnny said nothing false, nor did he have to remember an elaborate alibi.

But suppose Mom noticed that he got home later than usual and asks him why. If Johnny covers the truth (that he was kept after school by the principal) by saying that he went over to his friend Joe's house and played Ping-Pong, he needs to remember that line and its implications. The next day, when Mom asks if Joe's sister is home from college, Johnny can't say, "How should I know?" He has to remember that he said he was there yesterday. Memory does improve with age and, as with many other abilities, by adolescence is as good as an adult's.

Successful lying requires plotting out more than one step ahead at a time; it requires various contingency plans. Concealment lies require less of this skill. Concealment only requires figuring out whether you are going to be asked directly about what you want to conceal. Conceal-ment might work with Johnny's problem, but if Debra smashed her mother's favorite vase, she can't expect not to be asked if she knows what happened to it when Mom gets home.

Telling a false story makes the greatest demand on the liar's ability to think strategically. Johnny should consider a number of things if his Ping-Pong story is to be credible. He must already have shown interest in Ping-Pong for Mom to believe he would want to go to Joe's house to play. Then he has to make sure Joe is someone he often spends time with. What is the chance that Mom might have stopped by Joe's house? Might Mom talk to Joe's mom on the phone that day, or any time soon after? It would be best for him to base his false cover story on a friend whose parents are not acquainted with his mom. If he can't credibly do that, he should plan a response if Mom says, "I talked to Joe's mother this afternoon, and she didn't mention you were there." He could be prepared to say: "Well, we got bored playing Ping-Pong, and went down to the store for a magazine." Such sophisticated planning matures with age. Some people are never very good at it, others exhibit the mentality of a chess player when they are six years old. But for most children, this develops as they grow older.

A successful liar considers the perspective of the target being lied to. Taking the role of the other person, considering what will seem credible or suspicious to that person, allows the liar to consider the impact of his own behavior on the target and to fine-tune and adjust his behavior accordingly. Johnny should realize that if he said he stopped at the library to take out some books, Mom might be suspicious because she knows he doesn't go to the library very often. He also might reject that story line if he remembers that Mom is very interested in books and might ask to see which ones he took out. Preschoolers aren't very good at this because at such early ages children don't realize that there is more than one perspective—theirs—on an event. They think every-one thinks the way they do. As they move toward adolescence, kids become much more able to put themselves in someone else's shoes.

To lie well a child must also develop language skills, using words to refer to things that are not actually present. Children must be able to modify their speech—from vocabulary to inflection to rate of speech to actual content—to suit the occasion, in particular to tune what they say to the target. These language skills develop quite early, sometimes as early as age four, although they are far from perfect at that age.[23]

A successful liar is a smooth talker, able to think quickly and invent plausible accounts when caught off guard. Even if Johnny had not pre-pared a response to his mother's inquiries, he should be able to impro-vise an answer quickly. Although some people are very adept at thinking fast on their feet and coming up smoothly with a credible reply, little kids are not. But this, too, improves with age.

Skillful lying also requires emotional control. A good liar has the ability to feign emotions he or she doesn't feel, to sound and look calm, interested, pleased, or any other feeling required for the particular lie. Equally important, the liar must be able to conceal signs of emotions that could betray him or her. Johnny might be angry at the principal, believing he had been singled out for disciplinary action. He might be afraid of being caught, knowing that his parents would come down hard on him for getting into trouble at school and for lying to them. Maybe he feels guilty about lying to his parents, or excited by the challenge of succeed-ing at it. Any of these emotions would have to be concealed, and a mask would have to be shaped to fit his line. Some of my own research on children found that this ability to control expression, like most other abilities, improves with age, and by adolescence reaches the same level of competency as found in adulthood.[24]

These abilities—memory, planning, taking the role of the other person, fast thinking and talking, and control of emotions—are all neces-sary for the child to grow into adulthood. Ironically, the abilities that make parents proud and pleased at their child's development are also the same abilities that will later enable the child to disappoint and deceive his or her parents.

Growing up and achieving independence means a child has the ability and also the responsibility to choose between truthfulness and dishonesty. When the child knows he or she can't get away with lies, there is not really much choice. The temptation exists only when children know they can succeed if they choose to mislead.

Independence means having control over the information about yourself that you disclose to others. Privacy means making the decision yourself about who knows what about you. Having such control—enjoying one's privacy—doesn't require lying. Just as parents often say to their children, in nicer or nastier words, "Hey, that's not your business; don't ask me about that," a child can at times also have the right to say the same to a parent.*

These observations about why adolescents lie parallel the psychoanalytic view of lying, which emphasizes the role of lying in establishing independence from the family. Psychoanalysts see lying not as unique to adolescence but as present throughout childhood. Psychologist Michael F. Hoyt writes: ". . . the child's first successful lie breaks the tyranny of the parental omniscience, i.e. the child begins to feel that it has a mind of its own, a private identity unknown to its parents."[25] Secrets, concealing information, Dr. Hoyt continues, is seen as playing ". . . a significant role in the normal development of ego boundaries and the concept of the self. . . . More generally, possession of a secret confers the sense of having something uniquely one's own, of being a separate individual."[26]

In addition to the changes in abilities, there are also changes in attitudes that make lying easier and more likely when children reach adolescence. Social conventions that were inviolate earlier now appear to be arbitrary. The early adolescent typically no longer accepts without question, or at all, the legitimacy of many social rules.[27]

---

*In reading this passage, my son, Tom, told me it was foolish for me to suggest any kid could say that. "If you say, 'You can't ask me about that,' your parents know you did *something* and you're going to get punished," he explained. Tom is probably right; most parents would assume that coming from their child that sort of retort is evasive and means some wrongdoing has occurred.

Anna Freud, Sigmund Freud's daughter and a child psychoanalyst, provided one of the most astute characterizations of the dramatic swings in adolescent attitudes. In *The Ego and the Mechanism of Defense*, she wrote that adolescents are

> . . . excessively egoistic, regarding themselves as the center of the universe and the sole object of interest, and yet at no time in later life are they capable of so much self-sacrifice and devotions. They form the most passionate love relations, only to break them off as abruptly as they began them. On the one hand, they throw themselves enthusiastically into the life of the community and, on the other, they have an overpowering longing for solitude. They oscillate between blind submission to some self-chosen leader and defiant rebellion against any and every authority. They are selfish and materially minded and at the same time full of lofty idealism. They are ascetic but will suddenly plunge into instinctual indulgence of the most primitive character. At times their behavior to other people is rough and inconsiderate, yet they themselves are extremely touchy. Their moods veer between light-hearted optimism and the blackest pessimism.[28]

From this perspective your adolescent may be totally trustworthy one day in one mood, and completely unreliable the next with the opposite mood swing.

Adolescents become more confident about their ability to mislead their parents and less afraid of being caught. As I mentioned earlier, almost all the children I interviewed said they had the experience of getting away with a lie when they were between five and seven years old. Though they do not succeed at every lie, they begin to learn that it is possible. And if they keep lying, they will learn they have an increasingly better chance of succeeding with each year. If there is less fear of being caught, one of the deterrents to lying is gone.

Adolescence is a transitional period, for both child and parent—a time when rules, obligations, privileges, and rights change, not just once but again and again as the adolescent achieves more independence. Conflicts are bound to arise between the parent's wish to increase a child's responsibility and yet not decrease supervision and protection. During this time I expect that guilt about lying decreases for many adolescents, partly because the adolescent no longer views the parents as omniscient, partly because (in our culture) the adolescent needs to establish independence from parents and parents' values.

Rejecting their parents' values is often part of the separation process. The opinions of their peers—not their parents—matter more. Whether there's a slight generation gap or a full-scale rebellion, many adolescents do not feel as strongly compelled to do and act as their parents wish. The adolescent lives in two rather unrelated worlds—that of his friends and that of the adults. There is some solace in remembering that not all adolescents are alienated from their parents. Recall, for instance, the study showing that boys who maintained respect for their fathers were less influenced to engage in antisocial activities with their peers. But even those who still seek parental approval may feel more entitled or impelled to live their own lives, and justify lying to achieve that end. Armed with that justification, the teenage liar will feel less guilty and, as we have seen, less inclined to tell the truth.

MORAL AND SOCIAL JUDGMENT

Many developmental psychologists have proposed that a child's capacity to make moral judgment proceeds through a series of stages. While these scientists have not specifically been interested in lying, their findings can help parents understand how children think about lying as either good or bad.

By far the largest body of work, and the most controversial, was done by Lawrence Kohlberg,[29] who built on the ideas of the Swiss psychologist Jean Piaget. Kohlberg presented children with moral dilemmas in which obedience to laws, rules, or commands of authority conflicted with the needs or well-being of others. Here is one of the dilemmas Kohlberg and many other scientists have used:

In Europe, a woman was near death from a special kind of cancer. There was one drug that the doctors thought might save her. It was a form of radium that a druggist in the same town had recently discovered. The drug was expensive to make, but the druggist was charging ten times what the drug cost him to make. He paid $200 for the radium and charged $2,000 for a small dose of the drug. The sick woman's husband, Heinz, went to everyone he knew to borrow the money, but he could get together only about $1,000, which was half of what it cost. He told the druggist that his wife was dying and asked him to sell it cheaper or let him pay later. But the druggist said, "No, I discovered the drug, and I'm going to make money from it." Heinz got desperate and broke into the man's store to steal the drug for his wife.

Kohlberg interviewed children of different ages, asking them what they thought was right. The issue was not how they resolved a dilemma such as Heinz's but how they thought about issues of right and wrong. Kohlberg argued that children's judgments about morality go through a series of stages, changing as they grow (see the chart below).[30]

If Kohlberg is correct, and many psychologists think he is, parents should be aware of these stages and where their child fits in. Using reasoning that is based on the stage your child is at will enable you to have more impact when explaining to him or her why lying is wrong.

Kohlberg also proposed two later stages, based on personal conviction in ethical principles. The person at this stage no longer believes that it is always right to abide by the rules, expectations and conventions of society. Instead, the definition of right is based on mutual agreement, and upon principles. These stages are rarely reached by adolescents, or even by most adults.

The ages listed for each stage in the chart are only rough guidelines. Not everyone reaches stage 4. Many adults never go beyond stage 2. Even when children or adults progress to stage 3 or 4, they won't always think in those terms. When they are feeling strong emotions, they may move back to an earlier stage.

Let's consider how children's attitudes about lying change at each stage, and how this knowledge will help you discuss lying with your child.*

	Age	What Is Right	Reason to Be Good
Stage 0	4	Getting my own way Fairness is my way	Get rewards and avoid punishment
Stage 1	5–6	Doing what you're told What grownups tell you	Not get into trouble
Stage 2	6–8	Do onto others exactly what they do to you	What is in it for me
Stage 3	8–12	Live up to others' expectations Please others	So others will think well of me and so I can think well of myself
Stage 4	12+	Fulfill obligations to society	Keep society from falling apart; be a good citizen

In O stage, preschoolers think mostly in terms of what they want, and whatever that is, is right. For them lying in itself is not bad if it gets them what they want. At this stage, let your children know that you are happy when they tell you the truth, and that you don't want your child to lie. However, don't expect to make great inroads in having them understand that lying is wrong.

Children in stage 1 are impressed by the superior power of grownups. They are a lot more cooperative, but the cooperation is based not on understanding the rules but on wanting to obey adults. This is the

---

*Since no one I know of has directly studied this area, my suggestions are based on my reading of the literature on moral development, and in particular upon Dr. Thomas Lickona's book *Raising Good Children*, which I highly recommend for practical ideas about how to use the research on moral development in raising children.

period when children believe you can always tell when they are lying. Let your child know you don't like it if he or she lies. At this point begin to make appeals based on the next stage, helping your child stretch and grow in their moral thinking. Explain how unfair lying is to the person who is lied to. Ask your child how he or she would feel if someone lied to him or her.

In stage 2 kids no longer think adults are always right. Their notion of fairness is the golden rule, an eye for an eye, tit for tat. It's hard for kids at this stage to see that lying harms anyone. Try to use their tit-for-tat thinking to explain to them what would happen to their family, friends, or school if everyone lied and cheated. Also, start reinforcing the reasoning that accompanies the next stage by making clear your own disappointment if your child lies.

In stage 3 the child wants to live up to the expectations of others. A period of conformity, this phase underscores what has been called the "good boy" or "good girl" morality. Teenagers in this stage care so much about the approval of their friends that other moral concerns may be weakened if they conflict with what they think their peers expect them to do. This is a time when a conscience emerges, in the sense that children are motivated not just to avoid punishment but to live up to their own self-image. Kids will lie at this age to avoid displeasing their parents, and to avoid ridicule and win approval from their peers. At this stage you can appeal to your child's concern about his or her reputation, explaining how terrible it is to have a reputation as someone who lies. You can also begin to appeal to stage-4 reasoning, explaining how society would be undermined if everyone lied.

Teenagers who reach stage 4 (and Kohlberg does not suggest that all will) become concerned with being good members of their community, school, or society. Now they may comprehend the real conflict between loyalty to a friend who has committed a transgression and obligation to a society threatened by that transgression. It is a time when you can emphasize what happens when trust is lost. That point should be made to younger children, but don't expect them to be able to understand it as easily.

Although I think it useful for parents to know about these ideas,

I must report that Kohlberg's proposal of stages in moral judgment has been criticized on a number of grounds. Namely, that they are biased toward Western children; that they are biased toward males; that they require a higher education and a course in moral philosophy; and that they are politically biased toward liberals. Critics say Kohlberg presents development as more fixed and orderly than it is.[31] Others have argued that even if the findings are correct, they tell us only what children say, not what they do.[32] Children may be no more likely than adults to practice what they teach. Development psychologist Augusto Blasi critically examined the evidence from many studies, concluding that one's level of moral judgment is related to one's moral behavior.[33]

Kohlberg never claimed, however, that the stage of moral development was the sole determinant of cheating. A person may know what is right and still not do the right thing because of other determinants. A study that illustrates how many factors influence cheating or lying, and the role of moral judgment in all this, examined male college students.[34] Drs. Carl Malinowski and Charles Smith set up a cheating situation resembling Hartshorne's and May's classic study of cheating that I described earlier. The subjects were given a stylus, which they had to keep over a continuously moving light. Their score was based on how long they were able to keep the stylus on the light. They were told their score was a measure of attention and concentration, skills necessary in many occupations. They were given false and unattainable high norms that were said to be those achieved by athletes and college students, and low scores said to be made by institutionalized children. The results on five practice trials convinced the subject that he was at the low end. The experimenter then provided the temptation to cheat by leaving the subject alone, telling him to record the time he kept the stylus on target for the next ten seconds. The subject did not know that the true time was being recorded in another room.

Most of the students (77 percent) cheated at least once, but those at a higher stage of moral development cheated less and later than those at an earlier stage. Of those who never cheated, all but one was high in moral judgment. Of those who scored lowest in moral judgment, 96 percent cheated.

Just as important in predicting cheating was how well the subject did on the practice trials. Those who did the best on the practice trials cheated less. This was consistent with Hartshorne's and May's finding that there was less cheating on school tests by children who scored high in school-related skills.

Responses to one survey question also predicted who would cheat. The men who said they generally anticipate feeling guilty when they consider doing something wrong also cheated less. But this answer was not as powerful a predictor as either stage of moral judgment or preexisting skill. Those scoring low on anxiety about taking tests, and those who scored low on needing approval from others, cheated less. But neither of these factors was as strong a predictor as the stage of moral judgment or practice skill.

This study shows there are many issues to consider in understanding why someone cheats. The stage of moral judgment is one—but not the only—factor. Just as important are factors that are specific to a particular situation, such as how well your abilities equip you to succeed without cheating. There is a relationship between the stage of moral development and actual moral behavior, but other factors play a part as well.

Parents should know that they and their children will not view lying and other moral issues in the same way. Children's attitudes about moral issues change as they grow, though not necessarily in the orderly fashion or the same terms that Kohlberg proposes. The important message is to understand how your child thinks about lying. Be a good listener, draw your child out. Use stories, and present dilemmas like the one about Heinz. Find out your child's frame of reference. If you respond within that framework, you will have a better chance of influencing your child.

Although the frequency of lying may be an exception, almost everything else about lying changes as children grow. Their understanding of the concept of lying, attitudes about when lying is wrong, their ability to lie without being caught, and their moral and social judgment all change as they grow up.

Two age periods seem especially crucial. One is somewhere around three or four, when children become capable of telling a deliberate lie. This is a good time for parents to begin to educate their children about lying. As we have seen, what the child can understand at this early age is quite different from what will be possible later.

Adolescence is the other crucial period. Some of the evidence suggests that lying, and the influence of peers, peaks in early adolescence and may then subside. Much will depend, I believe, on how well parents handle their adolescent's needs for privacy, and whether they can grant their adolescent ever increasing power and responsibility over new areas of his or her life.

CHAPTER FOUR

A Teenager's Views on Lying

by Tom Ekman

"Face it. Your kids are going to lie to you until one of you dies."

Although I had interviewed many adolescents, I always wondered how much of what they told me was tailored for my ears. I thought I knew my son, Tom, well enough to believe that he would not censor what he thought, so I asked him to write this chapter. He was fourteen at the time. Adolescence is such a difficult period for both children and parents that I thought the unexpurgated perspective of a teenager on the subject of lying would be a rare opportunity from which we all would gain some understanding.

I did not tell him what to write, nor had he read any of what I had written. I did give him a short list of questions to consider. Given the fact that Tom was in no way directly influenced by me, it's reassuring to me that many of his ideas are quite consistent with my own, such as his theory that avoiding punishment is a major motive for lying in both children and adults. Tom's analysis of why bright kids lie less also fits with the findings I described earlier about brighter kids not cheating as much on school tests. Also, as he notes, in adolescence kids lie to gain privacy. And the enormous pressure to maintain social status can lead to lying.

While some run-on sentences were shortened and others edited to improve the grammar, all the words and ideas are his own. I have added some comments on his points at the end of the chapter.

I think you will agree that Tom writes well. He is considering a career in journalism. Though some of his insights may make you forget he is fourteen, occasionally one of his bolder defenses of lying will jolt you into remembering his age.

—Paul Ekman

It was the summer of '86 and I had just gotten out of eighth grade. My friend from London, Lucien, was with me and we were both going to a sailing camp within walking distance of our summer house in Inverness, a small community on Tomales Bay. The camp was a day camp, and as might be expected we sailed during the day. At night the kids of the camp, from about thirteen to eighteen years of age, would go out and party. We were the youngest of the bunch. It was during summer and my dad would work from Wednesday through Monday in Inverness, going back to his office in the city Tuesday morning and coming back Wednesday morning, so on Tuesday nights we were alone. (My mother was staying in the city during this time, while my dad stayed mostly in Inverness except for that one night a week.) As you will see, we were not old enough to handle the responsibility.

It all started one day when Lucien and I were telling the other kids about our new Jacuzzi. I decided then to have a party on Tuesday night, when my dad would not be home. My reason for wanting to have an unchaperoned party was that if my parents were there people would feel restricted, especially about drinking, and I knew my parents would never allow the older people to bring beer.

The party was great, and no one actually brought any beer. People came and had a Jacuzzi and went in the house, and it seemed to me that I was scot-free because nothing had been damaged and the neighbors had not complained about noise or anything. The next morning guilt set in, and I was worried about getting caught. I told Lucien that I would confess the second my dad got home. But when he arrived he was in a terrible mood, brought on by work stress, lack of sleep, and the fact that we had neglected to do our chores. I was too scared to tell him then, and decided I would tell him later, but I never got the nerve up. I never actually lied to my dad, but someone at the party had broken a hundred-dollar wooden duck without my knowledge, and when my dad asked me how it happened, I said I did not know, deceiving him, as I knew it had to be someone from the party.

A week passed and I thought I would get away with my secret party, but my parents found out from other parents about it, and were shocked that the kids who had been at the party had told their parents that my parents had been at the party out of sight. The punishment was pretty bad, but by far the worst part was that I still am almost never allowed to stay home alone anymore.

My parents were shocked that I had had the party. They did not think that I was capable of such deception. They were also mad because they had offered for me to have a Jacuzzi party with them around and then I went and had one when they were not there. They felt embarrassed when other parents found out that they had left two thirteen-year-olds alone and they had had a party, and felt irresponsible. In their eyes my image had drastically decreased, and they felt that I could no longer be considered as responsible as I had seemed to be. They liked to give me freedom and felt it was great that I could handle it, but after the party they were worried that they had been wrong about allowing me so much freedom.

The main difference in the way that my parents and I saw the lie lay in the loss of trust. When I told the lie, I of course considered the consequences if I was caught for my lie. I figured that my parents would be mad about the fact that I had had the party, the involvement of alcohol, the mess, etc. I thought that I would be punished and never allowed to stay home alone again, but in the excitement of having the party and all, I pretty much overlooked it.

My parents saw the lie in a totally different way than I did. Their anger at my having an unchaperoned party was nothing in comparison to their anger at the fact that I had deceived them. To them this was far more serious than anything else because I had abruptly done something that they did not think I would do and then deceived them about it. This shows how differently child and parent can view a lie.

For a kid, lying is about the same as it is for an adult. Giving one party misinformation to avoid, accomplish, fool, put down, or gain is the same for kids as adults. But as you can see from the story above, adults and kids can see lying in different ways. The difference really depends on the lie itself, as you will see as you read on.

WHITE LIES

The only category of lying that I think is virtually the same for both kids and adults is white lies. What I consider a white lie is a lie that benefits someone and is intended to have no major repercussions. Often these kinds of lies are told in order not to hurt someone's feelings, such as telling someone that you like their clothes when you really do not. As far as I can see, this protective lying is just as common for adults and kids, unlike other types of lies.

I think that just about any lie that is told to make a situation easier to deal with or one that benefits someone is a white lie. These include small lies about not emptying the dishwasher or why you're not in a good mood. For instance, often when I come home from school after a bad day, I will be in a bad mood and depressed and will not feel like talking to anyone. When a parent asks what is the matter, I sometimes will lie in order to avoid a confrontation, and say it is nothing or something small. A white lie is not serious in the telling, but can potentially become serious if found out. For example, lying about emptying the dishwasher is not a serious lie unless you are a repeated offender of not emptying the dishwasher, or of repeatedly telling lies about emptying the dishwasher. In that case the lie would become serious, as it might involve some repercussions on the parents' part in the form of punishment or a reprimandation.

SOCIAL LIES

After white lies come the whole range of social lies, which are often more serious forms of white lies. In many cases, this type of lying is more serious when used by adults, such as in cases of infidelity. Obviously, the more important and strong the relationship between a man and a woman, the more serious lies about infidelity are going to be. Although during high school years many teenagers become seriously involved in relationships, on the whole these relationships and any lies involved in them could not be nearly as serious as in the case of adults, where the problems become more serious with more sex and the added factor of marriage and children.

Almost everyone I know would agree that they are a lot more honest and truthful to their best friends of the same sex than to a boyfriend or girlfriend. But many would also say that they are more honest and truthful with their boyfriend or girlfriend than their normal friends. Thus, it seems that the order of importance of honesty in social situations begins with best friends, then boyfriends or girlfriends, and finally normal friends. All my better friends agree that no girl is more important than our friendship, and if it were to come down to a choice between their girlfriend or their better friends, they would drop the girlfriend. This actually happens a lot.

Recently I introduced one of my friends to a girl and it turned out that they both liked each other a lot. For some reason, though, the girl (who I had been good friends with) turned on me and started being really bitchy. My friend and I were not sure why she was doing this, but we knew that it had something to do with the growing relationship between my friend and her. Although I would have liked to see them get together, my friend knew that that would hinder our relationship. Because of this he decided to forget the girl because he felt my friendship was more valuable, for which I am still grateful.

Last year during school, a friend at my school took infidelity to the extreme, cheating on his girlfriend with three other girls! It is a little bit hard to pull that off and not get caught, but for weeks before his girlfriend found out for sure, he constantly lied and denied her suspicions with lies. When his girlfriend found out, it was all over, and his girlfriend was not especially pleased to find out that he had lied to her about the whole thing.

Social lies that do not involve relationships often involve exclusion in some part. For kids, who your friends and enemies are is very important, and there is a lot of social grouping and cliques (this goes away with age). Unavoidably, where there is social grouping and cliques, some kids are going to get left out. This often creates lies such as ones told in an attempt to keep someone out of a group.

I remember one day a few years back when some friends and I were on the bus planning Mike's birthday party. Suddenly we noticed that someone whom Mike did not want to invite was standing next to us. "Who's having a birthday party?" he asked. With hardly a moment's hesitation I proceeded to create a lie to cover up the situation. "Uh, well, you see," I began, "we were planning how to crash my sister's birthday party, but now we have decided that it would not work." This lie stuck in my head because later the person I lied to found out about the party and the lie and felt really betrayed by me. When a white lie like that makes someone feel bad, it can no longer be called a white lie because it is more serious and therefore, as in this case, should be called a social lie.

Regardless of the fact that adults probably lie more in relationships involving marriage, adultery, and children, kids still account for more social lying, simply because kids lead a much more social life. When kids mature and become adults, they lose a lot of the peer grouping and cliques of childhood. Adults still worry somewhat over their friends, but the general attitude seems to be that friends will come and go and one can always make new friends, so there is no need to get upset about matters with friends. On the other hand, kids in school tend to get extremely involved in friendships and cliques. A major part of every teenager's life is his or her social status, how many friends he or she has, whether he or she gets put down often.

At a summer family camp that our family recently went to, I noticed this happening. Because it was our first year we did not know anyone, and everyone else seemed to have been there for many years and knew each other. Because all the veteran campers knew each other, they stuck together in groups. This held true for adults as well as kids. On the first night, my sister and I felt a little bit left out, as we did not know anyone and everyone else was having a great time partying. My parents were not doing much better, so out of curiosity I asked them if they also felt left out. Interestingly enough, they did not seem to care. They said they were not worried about making friends because they already had plenty and they would probably never see any of these people again. Also, they had each other, so it did not make a difference to them. I think that this is a good example of how different an adult's and a kid's reaction are under the same social circumstances.

As for pre-teens, I think somewhere between about fourth and sixth grade, they start to think about how they fit into their peer group socially. Lies told that young are less serious, simply because at that age (and earlier) kids still don't understand all the potential applications of lies, and their parents are telling them not to lie. I think that social lying at that age does exist, just to a lesser degree because the children are not capable of telling serious lies.

I remember a time in fifth grade when some friends and I called up a girl and one of us asked her to be his girlfriend. She refused and hung up on us, but the next Monday at school, we told everyone that she had said yes. The purpose of our lying was to ridicule her. Although I think back on it as a childish prank, when it happened it seemed like the funniest thing in the world to ridicule this girl through our lying.

AUTHORITY-RELATED LIES

The biggest difference in lying between adults and kids is when it comes to lying to authoritative figures. Once again, the reason that kids lie more in this situation results from the fact that they get into these situations more often than adults. To a kid just about all adults are authoritarian figures in some way or another. To an adult, the thing that most often characterizes a person with authority is higher financial, business, or social status. To a kid, it's usually age—the authority is older than you.

The reason relationships involving authority relate to lying is that generally these types of relationships involve a lot of scrutiny of the inferior side of the relationship from the superior side. Because much of what the inferior party does in this relationship is questioned, watched after, and regulated by the superior party, the opportunity to lie comes up often. The inferior party lies about what he has done and the superior party (although much less often) lies to pacify the inferior party or to create an incentive for the inferior party to fulfill a duty, whatever it may be.

Another common reason adults lie to children is to cover up something or to keep the kids from knowing something they are not old enough to know or should not know about. This is a form of protective lying.

A friend of mine was to stay home alone overnight. His parents were worried about his having friends over—which he was not allowed to do and which he did without their permission the last time they left him home alone—so they made up a lie to keep him in line. They told him that they had asked the next-door neighbor to watch over him and if he had some people over she would find out and tell the parents. The kid knew he could not pull anything off, so he followed his parents' rules. He went out that night and came back alone. After a while, he realized that the family dog was not around. After searching for half an hour and not finding the dog, he decided to call someone and ask what to do. His parents had told him to call the police in an emergency, but he didn't think this was important enough, so he decided to call the next-door neighbor that his parents told him would be home. He reached her answering machine and it turned out that she was really in Lake Tahoe! He found the dog later on with another neighbor, but he felt really betrayed by his parents because they had lied to him to keep him in line.

Why is all this business about authority relationships so important to the way that kids lie? Because the two main authority relationships that kids have are parent/child and teacher/student. These two relationships, especially the parent/child, create more situations in which kids lie than all others combined. Adults have similar relationships, but the whole authoritative relationship thing diminishes as a person grows older. Adults may still have to deal with their parents, but this creates much less lying at that age because they see them less and live separately. This situation could also create lying, as it would be hard for the parents to find out if their child is lying, but the diminished contact really would take out all the lies that result from everyday contact.

The other type of authoritative relationship, teacher/student, also diminishes through age. For an adult, this is transformed into the boss/employee relationship. In both relationships the individual is dealing with someone who could make life easier or more difficult for him. This alone creates a superior/inferior relationship, and for kids add to that the age difference. The boss/employee relationship has the superior/inferior aspect to it, but the age factor almost totally disappears because of the fact that boss/employee relationships are between two adults.

LIES TO PARENTS

Why do kids lie to their parents so much? Mainly because parents are always looking out for their kids' well-being and always watching what they do. Often kids are trying to cover something up, something that would get them in trouble. I think that most lying to parents is aimed at avoiding punishment, a lecture. What they are trying to hide could be anything worthy of getting punished for. Naturally this kind of lying often involves drugs, sex, getting into trouble. Probably the thing lied about most commonly, though, is school. This is because all kids have to go through it and it is very important to how well the kid will do in life; obviously, the parents will be very concerned and full of questions. This just creates a great situation for lying because often the parents' limited contact with the school will make it impossible to disprove what their child is saying.

A friend of mine was having trouble in one of his subjects at school. After his parents saw how badly he was doing on his first-term report card, they got very angry. They threatened to punish him and take away privileges if he did not bring his grades up. The parents said that if the next report card did not show improvement, they would punish him fully. But even with his parents' threats, he continued to do badly.

Finally grades came around, and he knew that his grade would not be any better. His parents seriously thought he was improving because every time they asked him about the class, he lied and said that he was doing well. He became so worried about what his parents would do to him that he stole the report card sheet for that class, forged a much better report, and intercepted the real one. When his parents saw the grade, they were overjoyed at how good he had made himself sound and actually rewarded him for it. I have lost contact with this friend, but I assume that sooner or later his parents will find out about his forgery, and when they do, I feel sorry for him. Through the buildup of everyday lying, he was forced to risk getting into even more trouble than he would have had to suffer through if he had not forged his grading sheet.

Besides that, I think kids lie about other things for which they would not get punished because they want to keep a little bit of privacy. There are things that kids want to keep to themselves, such as things that they are embarrassed about, things that they are ashamed of, and things that they simply do not want their parents to know about. I know for a fact that most kids do not tell their parents much of anything about their relationships with the opposite sex. This is usually due to the fact that most kids would either be embarrassed or ashamed to talk to their parents about these matters, so they resort to lying. For a long time I did not tell my parents what kind of stuff goes on at our parties. This was not because I thought that I would get punished, it was just that I wanted to avoid any lectures and I just did not feel like telling them the truth.

LIES TO TEACHERS

Kids lie to teachers for many of the same reasons that they lie to their parents, but there are also some differences because kids have a different relationship with their parents. Parents have to be dealt with constantly, and they will be around for most of your life, so if you lose their trust you could have to live with it for a long time. Teachers, on the other hand, only stay with you for a term to four years, so they are lied to differently than parents. Unlike parents, who see you constantly, you see teachers only once a day during school, and generally kids try to make a better impression on them during class because they're grading you based on your performance once a day for forty minutes.

I think most kids are more reluctant to lie to their teachers than to their parents because teachers are harder to talk to if you get caught and, after all, the teacher is responsible for grading you, which gives him/her a lot of power. Still, since teachers are always checking on their students (like parents check on children) there will always be some deceit on the kids' part just because of the superior/inferior relationship that arises between students and teachers.

Obviously, the main things that kids lie to teachers about are related to schoolwork. This includes lies about homework, cheating, and work done in school. There is also a lot of lying about tardiness, behavior in school, and behavior out of school. All these types of lies result in a lot of lying at school.

I personally never cheat on tests in school. It's too risky, you could get kicked out of school. But I have cheated, as everyone else does, on quizzes because I know they don't really count and that I won't be punished by the school if I'm caught.

This could be turned around and looked at in a different way. People might think that kids would be less reluctant to lie to teachers than parents because the consequences will only last for the duration that the student has the teacher, as opposed to the fact that with parents it could last to their death. I don't think this is true. If a kid lies to the teacher, it might be reflected in grades, which affect the kid's future life. However, with parents respect can be won back, and the kid has so much time to make amends.

Just about everyone I know has lied about homework many times. It's just a given, especially because the teacher usually does not have time to figure out if you are lying or not. And just about everyone I know has lied about cheating and work done in school. The kind of thing that went on in our science class last year constantly combines all three of the aforementioned student/teacher lies into one lie-filled period. First, our teacher would ask for homework. Many would lie and make up fake excuses like not finishing the lab, forgetting the book, or some other creative story. Then, when class ended our teacher asked us if we had taken down the class notes. Everyone would say that they had and then copy them later!

IS LYING WRONG?

I have just written many pages about kids' lying. But is it right to lie? What I have written does not intend to encourage lying, it merely explains it.

Is it wrong for one party to intentionally communicate false information to another party in order to achieve something? The overall consensus of kids and adults is that some types of lying are good and some are bad. The question is: Where do you draw the line? I think all kids and adults will agree white lies are good. Almost everyone, kids and adults, tells white lies often. They may be told consciously or even unconsciously through habit. When someone asks me if I like what they are wearing, usually I will say yes without even thinking about it. If we did not have this type of white lie, there would be a lot of hurt feelings. The purpose of asking a question like the aforementioned is not so much that it's an honest request for a comment on the clothes he/she is wearing; it's more of asking someone for an ego boost because the person most likely expects you to say you like it, even if it means lying.

Kids feel little to no regret about telling these kinds of lies, as long as they are used for a good purpose. Being used for a good purpose does include trying to avoid getting in trouble. Kids tend to approve of lying about things like how late one stayed up. If the lie works and keeps the kid out of trouble, then what is wrong with it? It is not hurting anyone, and goes with the old saying about what you don't know won't hurt you. This mode of thinking seems to hold true for kids' reasoning for all types of lying: as long as it doesn't hurt anybody, what is so wrong about it?

In a relationship, lying is frowned upon. Although most kids admit that it may be necessary to lie in a relationship, it is thought that there should be little lying and the boy and the girl should be honest with each other. This is because in a relationship the boy and girl are supposed to be faithful, true, honest, and other things that run along those lines.

Because there are actually these unwritten "rules" that are supposed to be followed in a relationship, it is better to lie to a friend than to a partner. The unwritten "rules" for being a good friend are almost nonexistent, so there is much less of a taboo about lying to friends. Still, everyone admits that there are often reasons to lie in a social situation, and as long as it is done without hurting anyone, it is considered okay. For example, what if a boyfriend lies to his girlfriend about seeing his ex- who came back for the weekend from boarding school? What if he went to see her and did not do anything with her? Then it is okay for him to lie because he is not being unfaithful, it would keep him from getting in a hassle and it would keep her from getting upset about something that doesn't matter. But if he did cheat on her and she found out, then unquestionably the lie was wrong.

Lying in school seems to have much less support from kids. Although many people feel the same way about it as most kids feel about white lying and social lying, there are also many who do not approve of it. This comes from the way our society is set up and the way kids are taught from birth that school is so important and what the teacher says must be listened to. With all this ingrown respect for teaching establishments and the teachers themselves, it is not surprising that many kids feel a sort of taboo about lying to teachers. Teachers also give out the grades, which gives them a lot of power and gains them respect.

But no one really respects school that much, so most kids do not see anything wrong with lying about minor things like homework or tardiness. However, as regards lying about cheating, breaking rules, and similar things, many kids seem to think it is wrong to lie to teachers because of their authoritative position.

The same does not hold true, however, for parents. Every kid in the world has lied to his parents many times. On the whole, kids seem to think that it is often necessary to lie to their parents and that it is okay to do so. Parents stay with you for life, not just until the end of the semester, and therefore it is impossible to always be on good behavior with them and not lie. Also, because kids know they have to lie sometimes, it becomes almost natural and okay to lie to parents. It sometimes turns into a little contest about how clever one can be and not get caught. This kind of thing is more dangerous with teachers; punishments only last a little while, grades last for life.

Small lies told to parents are not even worth going into, because they are so common and all kids agree that they are all right to tell. Bigger lies, like ones about drugs, sex, and school, are much less common and much less supported by kids. Most of the kids that I talked to about telling big lies were divided or uncertain about telling big lies to their parents. Many said that sometimes it is necessary and some said that it should not be done often and is not good. It seems that there is about a fifty-fifty split in opinion about whether telling big lies to one's parents is okay. If I must stereotype the type of people representing each view, I'd have to say that the people who said that telling big lies to parents is sometimes necessary were generally the more social people who do not get good grades. I attribute this to the fact that people who do not do very well in school are more accustomed to lying, because of the things they do with their friends and because they have to lie about school more.

It is hard to define any type of lying that does not fit into white lying, social lying, school lying, and the child-to-parent lying category. The first thing that comes into my mind when I think about lying in this none-of-the-others category is lying to the ticket vendor at a movie theater. This sticks in my head because I've done it so often. All the kids I know see nothing wrong with it, and their excuse is that the theater already makes enough money so it doesn't matter. My parents completely disapprove and say that there is no reason for it; we have the money, they say, and we don't need to lie.

TIPS TO PARENTS

Face it. Your kids are going to lie to you until one of you dies. There is no way to avoid it. You have been lied to in the past and you are going to be lied to in the future. For a parent, there is little that you can do to avoid having your kids lie to you. As I said before, with the kind of superior party/inferior party relationship that comes from a parent/child relationship, there is no way to avoid lying. If you want to stop your child's lying altogether, tough. If you want to try to discourage your child from lying, read on.

I am afraid that I have no miracle solution as to how to stop kids from lying. For the most part it is unavoidable, and there will be lies that you could not have stopped. But if you create more situations where your child feels less compelled to lie and can tell the truth, then you can make a big difference as to how much your child will lie.

I think that white lies should be ruled out immediately as a part of this section. As for social lies, school lies, and any other kind of lie where your child is lying to someone else besides you, it is hard to keep your child from lying. Often you will have no way of knowing that a lie was told in the first place. The only thing that I can think of to keep one's child from lying outside the homestead is just to do what you have probably been doing all along, lecturing your kid on what is right and wrong. Now I cannot tell you exactly what you should teach your kids, but, although we all hate it, the best way to teach a kid something and make it stick is repetition. From a young age, you should begin teaching your child whatever your ideas are about lying if you want to keep them from lying. Although many kids in America are going to hate me for saying this, the truth of the matter is that repeated lecturing does work and is effective.

Lies in the home are something that, unlike the aforementioned type of lying, you do have control over. Although you can somewhat prevent this type of lying through lecturing, you also have the twin powers of questioning and punishing.

Questioning should be conducted calmly and not with an angry voice. I have been afraid to tell the truth sometimes to my parents, just because they are in a bad mood and are making me feel intimidated and not wanting to tell the truth. Although previous to the questioning and after it, I would probably rather confess and rid myself of the guilt and consequences, by then I am usually just trying to save myself at that exact moment and I'm not giving thought to possible repercussions.

A useful technique that will often bring out the truth is plea bargaining. Offering to lessen the punishment if the kid confesses instead of continuing the lie can be very tempting for the kid, especially if he/she has doubts about the credibility of his/her lie. Also, I think it works better to start the questioning out on small things, so your child is not tempted to make up a great big lie about everything, just because the first question scared him/her. If you suspect your child of drinking, do not straight-out ask him/her, "Have you been drinking?" Take it slow, and start by asking things like, "Where have you been?" and "What did you do?" If you question calmly and reasonably, your child will feel much less need to lie.

Although this will also gain me much hatred from many kids in America, I am going to reveal my parents' best punishments, which can be used as a deterrent to lying. When I was younger and my parents caught me lying, they would make me write from fifty to five hundred times the same sentence over and over. I WILL NOT LIE TO MY PARENTS. I WILL NOT LIE TO MY PARENTS. I WILL NOT LIE TO MY PARENTS. . . . This proved to be pretty effective, because I hated doing those lines so much. Now that I am older, my parents' two favorite punishments are to fine me or make me do work for them unpaid. Believe me, all three of these techniques work, and if used as a punishment/deterrent for lying, I can guarantee their effectiveness.

With the proper amounts of lecturing, questioning, and punishment you will not be able to stop your child from lying entirely, but you can make a big reduction in the amount, seriousness, and frequency of their lying.

Paul Ekman comments:

It is still hard for Tom to understand that having a secret party and not telling us afterwards was a lie. But the important thing he told is how my irritable mood made it hard for him to confess what he had done. I don't think he thought up the excuse afterwards. Dr. Thomas Lickona has written that "fear of a parent's anger is no doubt the single biggest cause of kids' lies. So, if you want your child to be truthful with you, try to minimize fear of your anger as an obstacle."[1]

My own father had an explosive temper with a very short fuse. He could be physically violent with little provocation. I've struggled throughout my life to keep that type of anger in check, and have never come close to violence. Tom's comments have helped me take another step away from my frequently angry reaction to his misdeeds. I cannot always prevent the anger, but I do somewhat better now in preventing my acting or speaking when I feel the anger. Tom has learned to remind me not to get angry or overreact, and I accept such advice with admiration for his ability to deal with me. Tom also has a short-fused anger. Sharing this problem has thankfully not led to battles, but to some understanding of what we must each contend with within ourselves.

On leaving the teenagers alone: I still do believe we made a mistake in placing that much temptation in front of two thirteen-year-old boys by leaving them alone overnight once a week.

On trust: In his first draft, Tom left out all mention of trust. When I asked him about the loss of trust, he reacted with surprise that he had forgotten it.

On inferior/superior relationships: Tom raises a point I did not consider about the difference in status between parent and child, between what he calls the superior and inferior sides. In the workshops I lead on lying, I often caution parents not to act like policemen. I ask how often they would lie if they had someone like a traffic cop living in their home, catching them every time they broke some minor rule.

On parental moralizing: Tom's plug for moral education was a surprise for me. My wife and I do take events from the newspaper once or twice a week and talk with the kids about the right thing to do. This is the first time he has let me know that he thought these sessions were of any use.

On "plea-bargaining": I disagree with Tom on this point. I think you should let children know that lying is almost always worse than the misdeed they are trying to conceal, and that you will be much more upset if they lie than if they tell you about it. But I don't think you should outright bargain about more and lesser punishments. Punishment won't always be an issue anyhow.

When I think Tom or Eve has done something they might be tempted to lie about, I try to remove that temptation rather than trap them into lying. I don't say, "I won't punish you if you tell me whether you did such-and-such." When I am quite certain one of them has come in way past curfew, rather than saying, "What time did you come in last night?" I'd say, "I heard you come in pretty late last night. What happened that you had to break your curfew?" If I am less certain, I might say, "Before you say anything, I want you to think before you reply to me. I think you might have come in way past your curfew last night. Please don't lie if you did; that would be much worse than breaking the curfew. But you know there is a reason for that curfew, and I have to know why you broke it."

CHAPTER FIVE

How Can Parents Cope with Kids' Lies?

by Mary Ann Mason Ekman

I asked my wife, Mary Ann, to write this and the next chapter because her background as a historian and as a family lawyer, and her authorship of a recent book on the status of women and children would enrich and add to the ideas I had planned for this chapter. The chapter builds on the research described in the earlier chapters, but adds also our experience and viewpoint as parents.

It struck me as a family law practitioner that this is a most confusing time to raise decent, moral children. It is not just drugs and TV violence that lead children astray. Family patterns have changed irrevocably. The prevalence of single-parent families and working mothers makes old patterns of raising children problematical. But do we have any new wisdom to replace them? Our traditional sources of advice and support, the community and the church, have been weakened in our increasingly urban and secular culture. We have many questions as parents, but few answers.

When I discovered that our son, Tom, then thirteen, had lied to us about throwing a party in our absence, my instant reaction was anger. As the anger subsided, my emotions shifted first to fear and then to guilt. My fear was that he might be turning the corner in the direction of serious teenage delinquency. There had been other indications of trouble at school: chronic lying about homework not done, classes cut and phony excuses proferred. Not one of these incidents was particularly serious, but clearly a dangerous pattern was developing.

As guilt gradually replaced fear, I began to examine my conscience as a mother. This was a child of a working mother who spent a large part of his early years in day care. This was a child who endured his parents' painful divorce at the sensitive age of four, and lived through the turmoil in my life until I met Paul and married again. In short, this was a child who experienced conditions of modern life that were commonplace for his generation, but uncommon for previous generations of children. Was I now seeing the frightening results of the way we raise our children now? (Later in this chapter I will attempt to deal with some of the special problems associated with lying and divorce. I will also examine the important influence of day care on the moral development of the child.)

I pondered his moral education We are not members of any religion, but surely we had taught him to be honest. We had spent many family dinners discussing lying and the effect it has on others. I recalled one or two incidents of lying in his childhood—they now seemed so innocent—when we forced him to write several hundred times, "I will not lie."

Then I reflected on our everyday life. Did we practice what we preached? The week following the disclosure of Tom's lie I carefully watched my own behavior. I caught myself telling eight lies, two of them to my children. They were the kind of lies that are not serious— in fact, most of them would not qualify as lies for many people. For instance, I told the vacuum salesman at the door that I had just purchased a new one. I told the meter maid that I had just run into the store for a moment. And I told my mother on the phone that I loved the blouse she had sent me for my birthday, which, in fact, I hated. The lies I told my children were, I thought, innocuous. I told my six-year-old daughter (to be humorous) that I was ten years younger than I am, although I don't usually lie about my age, and I told my son that when I was a teenager my curfew was ten-thirty, when in fact I couldn't remember when it was.

These were all simply lies of convenience. I gained little or nothing from telling them, and I could easily have told the truth with very little consequence. These were lies I didn't need to tell. Even worse, I didn't even realize I was telling them until I focused on my own behavior.

PARENTS' LIES

Perhaps the first thing that parents should consider when troubled about their children's lies is how prone they are to lying themselves. Those little lies of convenience, the so-called white lies, may mean little to adults. But children, who have a less sophisticated perspective, probably view them as real lies.

Parents are indeed the most important life model to the child, surpassing even the all-powerful teacher, who disappears with the advent of summer vacation. Researchers consistently find that one of the major predictors of which children lie is the behavior of the parents regarding lies. Drs. Hartshorne and May, in their extensive study on kids' lies, which Paul described in chapter 2, found this to be true. Two other studies have corroborated that children who lie most often come from homes in which parents also lie or otherwise endorse breaking rules.[1] The parents do not have to be engaged in criminal behavior. Everyday venalities, like cheating on your income tax or lying to the highway patrol when pulled to the side of the road, do not encourage a truthful child.

And parents must consider how often and in what ways they lie to their children. Aren't lies to children sometimes justified? Wouldn't the magical experience of childhood be dulled without the excitement of Santa Claus and the Tooth Fairy? Isn't it a kindness to a child to offer him a gentler explanation than the real one in a messy divorce?

To protect our children from what we as adults consider the harshness and unfairness of the world, we often lie to our children more often than necessary. Santa Claus and the Tooth Fairy can be valuable fantasies of early childhood, as are the bedtime stories and songs. At some point, however, usually between the ages of four and six, according to developmental psychologists, a child needs to sort out reality from fantasy. We must oblige the child, and not try to maintain the fantasy.

During this critical period from four to six the child becomes able to understand much more. This is the parents' opportunity to establish a lifelong habit of forthrightness. A child can learn that good deeds are not always rewarded, that parents sometimes fight or make mistakes, and that kids do not always come first. Some parents will choose to be honest about death when it strikes someone in the child's life. A child should be able to deal with the distressing fact that death sometimes comes too early, or with great pain. Dealing with the divorce of the parents is a more difficult matter, which I will deal with later in this chapter. Unfortunately, this most critical of all events for parents to relate to children occurs when parents have the least resources for handling it.

Bruno Bettelheim, in his revealing work on traditional fairy tales, *The Uses of Enchantment,* points to the value of exposing children to the conflict between good and evil. He explains:

> Contrary to what takes place in many modern children's sto-
> ries, in fairy tales evil is as omnipresent as virtue. In practi-
> cally every fairy tale good and evil are given body in the form
> of some figures and their actions, as good and evil are omni-
> present in life and the propensities for both are present in
> every man. It is this duality which poses the moral problem
> and requires the struggle to solve it.[2]

As our modern children's tales emphasize the sunny aspects of life and avoid topics like death or aging, modern parents often want to protect their children from real-life situations that are not pleasant. Protecting them with sugar-coated white lies, however, often raises rather than reduces the child's anxiety. A child who sees a parent or grandparent in pain does not need to hear that everything is just fine, the child already knows that it isn't. Instead, the parents should give the child more information to help him deal with his anxieties about a very real problem.

But parents can be forthright without revealing details that may be inappropriate for the age of the child. To a young child who learns of the rape of a neighbor girl, it is far more forthright to say, "Janie was hurt. The police will find the man who hurt her. When you are older, we will explain more about what happened to Janie," than to say, "Janie is in the hospital because she got sick."

PRIVACY

Six-year-old Jimmy occasionally experienced nightmares, "night monsters" he called them. He was in the habit of crawling into bed with his mom and dad when they occurred. One night their bedroom door was locked. In the morning he angrily accused his mother of locking him out. Flustered, his mother, Alicia, who did not want to admit they had locked the door to make love, told Jimmy that it was a mistake and would not happen again.

At this critical age between four and six a child can also learn that he does not have to know everything. Adults have areas of privacy that are off-limits to children. Very often this restricted information relates to sex, but it could also deal with family scandals, or neighborhood gossip. Parents certainly have the right to lock their bedroom door. When questioned, they can explain that parents have certain activities that are private and for adults only. This does not mean parents should keep sex a secret. There is agreement among developmental psychologists that children should be gradually educated about sex from the first moment they can formulate a relevant question. Of course, a four-year-old does not require the detail offered to a fourteen-year-old. But neither the four-year-old nor the fourteen-year-old need an explanation of their parents' sex life—for most families an area of parent privacy.

Privacy is a two-way street. If parents want to discourage lying, they must not only be frank about their own need for privacy, they must extend the courtesy to their children. One of the greatest strains between parents and children is the child's ever-increasing need to become independent, and therefore more secretive, and the parents' equally strong but opposing need to protect, control, and guide. It has become part of the accumulated wisdom of this culture that this tension regularly erupts into full-scale combat with adolescence. There are, however, occasions for conflict about privacy throughout childhood.

Kids very often lie to parents to protect what they consider their private life. When a seven-year-old comes home from a birthday party, she will probably respond happily and honestly to her mother's questions about who was there, what they had for lunch, and what games they played. At fourteen, this same child may well respond sullenly, evasively, or with outright lies. The lies and evasions may occur because she believes her mother will disapprove of the honest answers, because she is asserting her independence, or they may occur because she feels it is not her mother's business.

Children by the sixth grade often live in two worlds: the world of their peers and that of their parents. According to the studies of Dr. Berndt, which are described in chapter 2, the peer world has a stronger pull on new adolescents than the parent world. Adolescents keep the division between these worlds by not talking about parents to their peers, and by not talking about their peers to their parents. An adolescent may view his parents' questions about his friends as a hostile intrusion into his private world.

But even the seven-year-old develops areas of privacy. She may not like being asked whether or not she has a boyfriend, and she may not want to be seen less than fully clothed by any males, probably including members of her family.

How can we protect and guide our children unless we know what is going on in their lives? Can we accept the standard "Nothing" reply to the daily question, "What happened at school today?" There is no easy answer to this universal parent problem. Every parent "needs to know" some information, but just how much depends on the age of the child, and on the parents' conception of their fundamental duty to protect and guide their child.

Let us take sex, a critical area of concern for all parents, accelerating as the child moves into adolescence. What do parents "need to know" about the sexual activity of their child? If parents have a right to privacy about their sex life, does the child have the same right to privacy?

The minimum that all parents "need to know" is the occurrence of sexual abuse. For a young child this includes the unauthorized touching or sexual assaults by adults or older children. (I will deal with the complicated controversy regarding lies and sexual abuse in the next chapter.) Parents are divided, however, about whether they "need to know" about kissing and touching between young children of the same age. Many parents will feel that this is innocent behavior, and a natural part of development. Others may feel quite strongly that they must protect their children from what they consider promiscuous behavior.

Parents will also disagree about what they "need to know" about the sexual activity of their adolescents. While all parents would agree that they need to know about sexual abuse in the form of force or violence, or exploitation by adults, many parents believe that beyond that they don't "need to know," and often don't want to know, the nature of their adolescents' sexual activity. Other parents feel quite strongly that they must protect their teenager from premature sexual activity. Therefore, they must know what, where, and with whom their children are engaged at all times. Some parents feel they must protect their daughters, but not their sons.

The issue is not what is right or wrong about parents' differing attitudes toward the sexual behavior of their children. In a pluralist culture there will always be different points of view about sex and other behavior in which children engage. The issue is whether the parent has carefully considered what he "needs to know" and what he can accept as a private area of his child's life. If it is an agreed-upon private area, the child has the right to remain silent or to say, "That is private for me," as parents do about their locked bedroom door.

Unfortunately, most parents live day to day, crisis by crisis. They rarely take the time to think through what it is they "need to know." Even more rarely do they discuss this issue with their child. A child may feel forced to lie about an issue, rather than say, "This is my private area." He doesn't realize he may have that option.

Perhaps as parents we can develop a "need to know" mental checklist, which we revise as the child develops. Such a checklist may include:

Behavior of friends
Whereabouts in free time
Information about friends
Behavior at parties
Snacking behavior
Television programs watched
Homework accomplished
Behavior at school

For older children it might also include:

Sexual behavior with peers
Use of drugs
Use of alcohol
Rides in cars with others
Behavior driving the car

Once we as parents have decided what we absolutely "need to know," we can make these areas clear to our child, along with our reasons for this need. At the same time we can make it clear that he still has areas of privacy where he does not have to divulge all. For instance, we may say that his telephone conversations and letters are his private concern. Some parents believe that their child's room is an area of total privacy, entered only with the permission of the child.

Ann, the mother of a fifteen-year-old boy, revealed to me, "His room was filthy, an absolute pigsty. He got furious every time I waded in to try to clean it. I got furious because he wouldn't clean it himself. We were angry with each other all the time. Finally I decided I couldn't stand the struggle and I just gave up. Now we can actually kid about it. It's still a pigsty, but we can talk to each other again."

Not all parents could live with this solution, but they could reach some compromise that would allow the child a realm of privacy.

LYING AND FRIENDSHIPS

Another critical area in which parents can encourage truthful children is monitoring the friendships of their children. Hartshorne and May observed, "In human affairs, birds that flock together acquire similar plumage."[3] They found that children who lie have friends who lie. In a classroom cheating situation, they observed that children who cheat (not by copying each other's papers) usually sit adjacent to other cheaters. More recent studies report that if a child sits near a cheater when taking a school exam, that child is more likely to cheat on the next exam.[4]

These scientific studies only support what parents have always known—bad friends can cause bad trouble for your child. Parents have always known this, but most parents feel helpless in controlling their children's friendships. This helplessness grows as the child grows older. And the older child is increasingly more susceptible to the influence of her peer group. My friend Martha, complaining about the poor behavior and poor grades of her thirteen-year-old son Ben, said, "I think a lot of his bad behavior is copying his friend Matt. I don't like Matt, I don't feel that he is acting straight with me. I know he lies all the time to his parents. But what can I do? If I forbid Ben to see Matt, he will see him anyway and just lie to me about it."

Martha's frustration is familiar to most parents. We cannot supervise our children twenty-four hours a day once they enter school. In the highly socialized world of the classroom and playground they will make friendship choices that we may not like but cannot control. As they grow older, these friendships become more and more important to them, often, it seems, more important than their ties to their parents.

How can we control our children's choice of friends? There is no easy solution here. Perhaps all we can do is to help our child develop into a self-confident and moral child who will attract friends of the same persuasion. Encouraging activities in which a child will excel will surely bolster the child's self-esteem and allow him to be less dependent on peer approval. Supporting activities like scouting or volunteer work that occupy free time and promote a sense of charitable contribution are invaluable.

I believe that a parent should know at every age who the child's friends are and what they are doing in their free time together. This may not be on every parent's "need to know" list, but it is on mine. I also believe that a parent has the right to tell the child he disapproves of a friend, but *only* if he has specific evidence about the friend's bad behavior. For instance, a parent should not disapprove of a friend because of his family, physical attractiveness, or color. A parent does have the right to disapprove of a friend if he catches the friend in a lie, or if the friend is suspended from school for cheating or stealing. A parent can forbid the child to see the friend upon pain of punishment, but a more successful approach may be to explain to the child exactly why the friendship may be destructive to him. Then the parent may promote new friends and new activities for the child.

There is, unfortunately, the sad situation in which a parent is unable by any means to separate a child, usually a teenager, from a friend or friends who continually lead her into trouble. The child may lie repeatedly to conceal the fact that she is still seeing this undesirable friend or friends. Perhaps the only hope in this situation is to remove the child physically to a different environment. Since it is unlikely that the parents can move, the child may be sent to the home of a relative or to a boarding school that maintains close supervision. This extreme solution provides no guarantee that the child will not make new, but equally undesirable friendships, but it may be the only way out of the deceitful and destructive pattern.

In many eras of Western history it has been common to send adolescents to live in the home of another. Most often this was a form of apprenticeship through which the child could learn a useful skill, such as homemaking or ironmaking. The incentive for sending the adolescent to another home was not only to learn a useful trade, but to put the child under an authority other than the parent.

TRUST

Perhaps the most important contribution we as parents can make to raising a truthful child is to develop a relationship securely founded on trust. This kind of bond does not arise from lecturing about a single lying incident, it is nurtured from the beginnings of communication between parent and child. In order to develop trust in a child, we must regularly demonstrate to the child that we trust him.

On Halloween night in 1986, Sandra Visnapuu received a call from the police, who said they were charging her fourteen-year-old son with vandalism, spray painting a house. They said there were two eye witnesses and there was no doubt. Disappointed and angry, Mrs. Visnapuu confronted her son, Neil, who said, "I swear, Mom, I didn't do it."[5]

This story was worthy of coverage in the *New York Times* because the mother not only believed that her son was not lying to her, she spent several weeks personally investigating the incident to find the truth. Mrs. Visnapuu went door to door in the neighborhood where the incident occurred, and talked to all of his friends. As a result of her efforts, the real vandal came forward, a fifteen-year-old boy from another neighborhood, accused of another incident on Halloween night. "The whole time, there were people who didn't believe us," Mrs. Visnapuu said. "Everybody—police, school counselors, even our lawyer—said that nine times out of ten times, a kid who says he's innocent is really guilty."[6]

This mother went to extraordinary lengths to show her son that she did indeed trust him. She had the confidence of fourteen years of parenting that her son would not lie to her.

How can a parent nurture this all-important bond of trust? First, a parent must deserve trust. A parent who lies to a child frequently, or who regularly does not live up to promises made, cannot expect that child to act any differently. A parent who relies on harsh punishments, or treats the child unfairly, may find that his child obeys out of fear, not respect.

A parent can reinforce the importance of trust with storybook examples like "The Boy Who Cried Wolf," and as the child grows older with examples from the news. A child can appreciate that lies told by public officials in scandals such as Irangate are a breach of trust with the public. He can learn that there are consequences for the breaking of trust.

Second, even a young child can feel proud and grown up if the parent lets him know frequently that he trusts him. A continually suspicious parent will not produce a truthful child. As the child moves toward adolescence and the parent fears he is losing control, there is too often a tendency for the parent to fear the worst. Therefore, the parent may jump on small pieces of suspicious evidence.

Sara, fifteen, came home from a basketball game and entered the living room to say good night to her parents. Her mother exclaimed with alarm, "Sara, your jacket smells like it's been in a fire sale—have you been smoking?" Sara quickly responded, "Oh no, Mom, I was sitting next to Tod, he smokes."

A parent who smells smoke on his child's clothes may be too willing to believe the child is smoking, even if the child offers a plausible excuse. In our courts of law the defendant is innocent until proven guilty. In the household family court, the adolescent defendant is too often presumed guilty and must prove himself innocent.

In this alleged smoking incident, the worst response a parent can make is to call the child a liar, and try to wrest a confession from him. The better approach is to tell the child that honesty is more important to you than smoking. If he was smoking he should tell you, and you would value his honesty more than you disapprove of an incident of smoking. If he still denies it, you should let it go. There may be other incidents (which I shall deal with later) where the stakes are much higher and you absolutely need to know the truth. One instance of suspected smoking, for most parents, is not that kind of incident.

Even when a child is caught in an outright lie, this should not be the end of trust. A parent can tell a child that although lying will affect the bond of trust, a single lie is forgivable. If the lies continue, the child, like the boy who cried wolf, will suffer the consequence of loss of trust. Our son, Tom, following the incident of the unauthorized party (preceded by other lies), lost the privilege of staying overnight by himself. And it will be restored only when trust is restored. A child may learn from such experiences that trust is important, and must be worked toward.

Chapter 3 demonstrates how the understanding of trust is a function of development. Very young children most often believe that the consequence of lying is punishment. Very young children are also unequivocal in their belief that lying is wrong. By ten or twelve, children shed their belief that lying is always wrong; they can begin to see the differences among lies, and begin to judge a lie by its consequences. For example, if you untruthfully tell a friend her hair looks nice it only produces a positive consequence. Tom, in his chapter, tells us that teenagers not only learn to tell white lies, they begin to tell what he calls "social lies" to manipulate their relationships with their peer group.

With adolescence, children can also begin to understand the consequences of lying other than punishment. The loss of the trust of a parent or friend is understood as a serious negative consequence. Most children cannot clearly express their understanding of the loss of trust as a main consequence of lying until mid-adolescence. Some children never understand this at all.

In his controversial theory of moral development discussed in chapter 3, Lawrence Kohlberg describes what happens to children at different ages. He claims that children from four to eight behave solely to avoid punishment when forced with an ethical choice, like stealing food for a sick person. Some adults never grow beyond this stage. In the early elementary grades the child may reason that looking out for oneself is the greatest motivation for behavior, but it is also important to be fair to those who are fair to you. A few years later, around junior high, a child may begin to believe that it is important to do good deeds in order to win the social approval of being a good person. Higher stages of moral development, which occur in late teens and early adulthood, include acting in conformity with legitimate authority—e.g., the law of your country—and at the highest levels, acting upon the conviction of your own ethical principles, which support a system that gives the greatest respect for the rights and dignity of every individual person.[7]

According to Kohlberg's theory, it is in the teen years when children realize that it is important to be a good person for the approval of others, including parents. During these years parents can more firmly establish the importance of trust in telling the truth that they have hopefully introduced in earlier years, and try to move away from fear of punishment. A parent may say (more than once, since repetition is essential with children), "Nothing is more important than trust between us. If you have done something that you know I will disapprove of, don't be afraid to tell me. Remind me not to get angry. You may have to do something to make up for it, but I will be very proud of you for telling me the truth."

Children who are not raised in an atmosphere of trust may have trouble ever viewing the consequences of their lies as broken trust. Particularly if they are raised with harsh punishment, they may continue to see lying at the lowest moral level of acting to avoid punishment. They will never approach the higher levels of seeing their actions as a citizen of their society, or ultimately as a citizen of the world.

CRIME AND PUNISHMENT

A parent can set a good example by being forthright and truthful to the child. A parent can give the child needed areas of privacy. A parent can monitor the friendships of the child. A parent can try his best to develop a firm bond of trust. But even the best of parents (and who among us can claim sainthood) may have to face catching his child in what appears to be an outright lie.

American parents place the highest value on honesty in their children. In yearly studies conducted by the National Research Center at the University of Chicago between 1972 and 1986, honesty consistently showed up as the single most desirable quality for a child to have. It was considered even more important than being a good student.

For many parents then, the act of lying becomes the major issue, not what the lie is about. A parent may well find himself uncontrollably angry toward a teenager who says she missed the curfew because her friend's car broke down (for the fourth time that month). He would accept more calmly the real explanation, that she was having a good time and didn't notice it was late.

How can a parent handle this common situation in a manner that will encourage future truthfulness and not simply provoke an angry confrontation?

TRAPPING THE LIAR

There is general agreement among experts who deal with children that engaging in a power struggle to obtain a confession is usually the worst tactic. As pointed out in chapter 3, there are clues to deceit in the face, voice and body, but a wise parent does not usually employ them to force a confession from his child. This advice runs contrary to the parent's strong urge to trap the child in his own lie.

A parent who screams: "You're a liar. I'm going to call Sue's parents right this minute and find out if her car really broke down. You can't tell me that same lie again!" surely succeeds in venting his own frustration. He certainly succeeds in provoking hostility and defensiveness on the part of his daughter. He may even succeed in proving his daughter a liar if he makes that telephone call. But does he succeed in teaching her a moral lesson?

It is not so simple. By uncovering her lie and responding with wrath, this father will probably provoke fear in his daughter. That fear may make the daughter think twice about lies in the future, certainly about lies relating to curfew. Her fear may make her an apparently more truthful child, or at least a more successful liar. His fury will also impress upon her how seriously her father takes lying. But can a father afford to develop a relationship with his daughter based on fear? Can a father afford to be a policeman?

Rather than focusing on trapping his child in a lie, the parent has a better chance of developing a trusting relationship if he focuses on the reason for the lie, the importance of the curfew. He might say, "I really don't want to hear any more excuses about why you are not home by your curfew. The point is, I need to know when you are coming home. I worry about your safety and I need to know where you are. If you are not going to be home on time, you must call."

The parent should then go further and point out, without forcing a confession, that he also needs forthright explanations from the child when a curfew is missed. That knowing he can trust the child's word is as important as knowing where the child is.

This second approach will not provoke fear in the child, but it may not produce the dramatic changes in behavior that may occur if her lie is uncovered in wrath. These are choices a parent must make. It is often more difficult to work toward a relationship of mutual trust and responsibility than to instill a fear of getting caught.

But let's face the fact that with some lying incidents the patient road toward developing trust and internalizing responsibility may not be possible. Sometimes it is essential to learn the truth, even if it means forcing a power struggle. Let us deal with the kind of lie that chills parents' blood.

Thirteen-year-old John has been acting strangely for weeks. He falls asleep frequently, even while eating. He no longer seems interested in basketball, his favorite sport, and has stopped talking to his friends on the telephone. During these weeks his mother twice notices that she has about twenty dollars less in her wallet than she expected. The first time she is short she dismisses it as her own error, the second time she is alarmed.

She asks John about the missing money. He claims innocence. She asks him why he is so tired. She suggests taking him to the doctor. He claims that he is having trouble sleeping because he has too much homework.

John's mother needs to know. She has good reason to suspect her son is in serious trouble, possibly with drugs, and she must play policeman in order to learn the truth. She knows her child, and she can look for the signs of deceit discussed in chapter 3 to corroborate her suspicions of lying.

To obtain a confession, she may first offer amnesty. She may promise that she will not punish him if he reveals all. She must be certain, of course, that she is willing to do so. Can she really let a serious theft go unpunished? If the offer of amnesty does not work, she may have to become a detective. She will talk to his friends and his teachers in order to learn the truth. She may feel obliged to search his room. She will confront John with evidence she obtains in order to wrest a confession.

John's mother must engage in a power struggle, she must play policeman because the stakes are so high. If her son has become a thief and a drug user, he needs help immediately. She cannot rely on building trust and responsibility as a strategy to deal with his lies.

It is the teenage lies that make parents frantic. Teenagers no longer accept without question the legitimacy of social rules and often feel justified in lying to avoid following scorned rules. As Tom tells us in his chapter, many of the lies teenagers tell do not involve parents at all. They are focused on gaining status in their other world, the world of their peers.

Developmentally, teenagers have become far more skilled at lying and are not as likely to get caught as younger children. They have better memories and more sophisticated intellectual powers to create a believable lie. They also can better control their nonverbal behavior. As their confidence in escaping detection grows, so often does the incidence of their lying. And sometimes their lies can be dangerous to themselves and others.

It is hard not to engage in a power struggle with a teenager when a lie is suspected. The act of lying itself enrages most parents, compelling them to force a confession at any cost. And, as noted in the example of John, the suspected thief and drug user, sometimes a power struggle is necessary. Most teenage lies, however, are not that serious. They deal with mundane issues such as homework not done, chores not completed, items of clothing lost or damaged. A parent must make a judgment on when to act as policeman and force a confession, and when to avoid a power struggle and focus on regaining trust.

How important is it to know the truth? For each parent the stakes may be different, but for all parents, suspected physical harm, as with drug use or suspected criminal activity, should be reasons for forcing the truth.

The same guidelines can be used in dealing with the lies of younger children. Concern over physical harm, as with issues of sexual abuse, or suspected criminal activity such as petty thievery, may justify a power struggle. Other lies should be dealt with in a less accusatory manner.

When our son, Tom, was nine we gave him five dollars to cover both admission at the Saturday afternoon movies and fifty cents' worth of candy. We asked him to bring back the change. He returned home with no change and said he had been held up outside the theater by a man with a mask. Upon further questioning it was clear that the alleged robber was a fiction, but Tom would still not confess that he had used this money for himself. In desperation, his coverup story grew more elaborate and fantastical.

We felt driven to make him confess. We called the boy with whom he had gone to the movies and learned he had spent the dollar on malted milk balls. We had pinned Tom into a corner, and finally he broke down sobbing and confessed. We had played policemen and won. But did we need to force this humiliation on Tom? Were the stakes so high that we needed a confession? Once we were confident that it was indeed a lie we could have spared him the final humiliation. We could have said, "It is very important that you don't lie to us. We need to trust you or we will not be able to allow you to go to the movies without us. We would worry about you too much. If you had not lied and told us you spent the money on candy, we would have given you only a small punishment."

This approach could have led to a dialogue about the importance of trust rather than the crying and sullen behavior that we in fact produced. We may have restricted his moviegoing for a week as well to reinforce the lesson of broken trust. But we would not have ended the confrontation as the triumphant policemen and the broken criminal.

Very often younger children's lies take the form of bragging or telling tall tales. Your son may tell you that he is the best hitter on the team, when you know he is barely keeping up; your eight-year-old daughter may claim she has five best friends, when you are certain this is wishful thinking. This kind of lie is often a call for help. Your child may be suffering serious feelings of inadequacy. For whatever reason, the child is seeking attention, and it is up to you to find out what is going wrong in his life. Although you should let him know that his boasts do not fool you, use his revelation as a gentle way to probe behind the boast.

TO SPANK OR NOT TO SPANK

Parents may learn to avoid power struggles and focus on the issue of trust rather than trapping the liar. But parents must still decide on appropriate punishment if they are certain a lie has been told and the crime deserves punishment. Appropriate responses to lying and to the offense it attempts to cover up are difficult for all parents. Discipline is an area where there are no clear guidelines. Most parents discipline their children as their parents did them, for lack of any other model.

Mary Bergamasco was arrested for child abuse in Hayward, California. She had dressed her seven-year-old son as a pig and displayed him on her Hayward lawn with a sign on his chest for passersby to read. The sign said: "I'm a dumb pig, Ugly is what you will become every time you lie and steal. Look at me sqeel [*sic*]. My hands are tied because I cannot be trusted. This is a lesson to be learned. Look. Laugh. Thief. Stealing. Bad Boy."

Mary responded that the boy had been stealing and lying like a hardened criminal. She said that her mother had punished her in a similar manner. "But," she said, "I didn't burn his hands like my mother did to me."[8]

The media picked up this story and the ensuing attempt by the boy's father, who had seen the boy only twice, to gain custody. The most interesting part of the story was the split in public opinion. Many thought it a heinous act, and others believed it was within the range of appropriate discipline. After all, they said, she had not physically hurt the child.

The experts have been almost as confused about appropriate punishment as have parents. There are, however, some scientific studies that clearly suggest that some parental responses are better than others.

Martin Hoffman and Herbert Saltzstein carried out an extensive study on seventh-graders in 1967 that measured the relationships between the types of parental discipline and moral development of the child. The child's moral development was measured by paper and pencil tests, by teachers, peers, and the child's own parents. The children and the parents then reported the kind of discipline they received at home. Discipline techniques were divided into three categories: power assertion, in which the parent asserted power and authority over the child; love withdrawal, which included forms of anger and disapproval, but no physical punishment; and induction, in which the parent focused on the consequence of the child's action on others.

Induction won handily over power assertion and love withdrawal.[9] This means that a child who is consistently told the effect his bad behavior has on others has a better chance of internalizing the lesson and not repeating the behavior. The child who is physically punished for his behavior, or who has love withdrawn, has less chance of incorporating the lesson. The father who explains why missing the curfew worries him has a better chance of inculcating the lesson of responsibility and truth telling than the father who blows up.

Even young children can be taught how lies to his parents, teacher, or friends will affect his relationship with them. A parent can appeal to the child's pride and desire to be thought grown up.

This evidence surely flies in the face of the "spare the rod, spoil the child" school of child raising, but in fact the experts have been moving rapidly away from that tradition. In the 1945 edition of *Baby and Child Care*, Dr. Benjamin Spock wrote: "I am not particularly advocating spanking, but I think it is less poisonous than lengthy disapproval, because it clears the air, for parents and child." In the 1985 edition of the book, however, Dr. Spock deplored spanking, saying it taught "children that the larger, stronger person has the power to get his way whether or not he is in the right." He even suggests that the "American tradition of spanking" might contribute to violence in the United States.[10]

Although there are a few dissenters, most child-care experts have now come to believe that parents must find alternative methods of earning a child's respect. As a consultant to the Connecticut Department of Children and Youth Services put it, "Most juvenile delinquents are raised on belts, boards, cords or fists."[11]

Most experts now believe that power-assertive discipline, which includes physical punishment and threats, is associated with a lower level of moral development. It creates a fear of punishment, rather than an internalized belief in moral behavior.

With lying, there is a consensus that a child who is subject to harsh physical punishment lies more often in order to avoid punishment. These children are not likely to develop to the stage where they reject lying because of the breakdown of trust or the consequences to others. They will always see lying as a strategy to avoid pain.

Parents, however, have not caught up with the experts. A 1984 survey by the University of New Hampshire's Family Research Laboratory found that 88 percent of parents polled spanked their children. Of those, 50 percent said they used physical punishment as a last resort, and 33 percent said they spanked their children when they felt frustrated or "out of control." Surveys conducted since the 1920s have shown much the same results.[12]

It is not at all surprising that parents do not follow the current trend among experts. In fact, physical punishment is as American as cherry pie. George Washington's father very likely spanked him, but still managed to gain good results in the truth-telling department. A study of colonial child-raising practices would make even the toughest advocates of physical punishment appear softhearted.

Our Puritan forefathers believed that children came into the world stained with sin, their passions powerful, and their intelligence weak. It was the role of the parent, particularly the father, to beat down their passions and to form their good character. This took constant vigilance and the strict control accomplished by physical punishment, often the whip. Since mothers were considered prone to indulgence and excessive fondness, it was the responsibility of the father to supervise their moral development. It was for this reason that the law gave custody rights to the father rather than the mother in cases of separation.[13]

John Wesley, one of the principal founders of Methodism, clearly expresses the eighteenth-century view of child rearing in his 1783 "Sermon on the Education of Children":

> To humor children is, as far as in us lies, to make their disease incurable. A wise parent, on the other hand, should begin to break their will, the first moment it appears. In the whole art of Christian education there is nothing more important than this. The will of the parent is to a little child in the place of the will of God. . . . But in order to carry this point, you will need incredible firmness and resolution, for after you have once begun, you must never more give way. You must hold on still in an even course: you must never intermit your attention for one hour; otherwise you will lose your labour.[14]

John Wesley believed that lying must be sternly quashed. "Teach them that the author of all falsehood is the devil, who is a liar and the father of it. Teach them to abhor and despise, not only lying, but all equivocating, all cunning and dissimulation."[15]

By the nineteenth century, attitudes toward discipline had loosened considerably, and the mother replaced the father as the principal moral educator of small children. This was in part a practical recognition that fewer fathers worked on the farm and were now likely to spend their days away at offices or factories. No longer were children seen as basically evil. The role of affection rather than discipline was stressed.

In a widely read book of the time, *The Mother at Home*, Congregationalist minister John S. C. Abbott advised:

Guard against too much severity. By pursuing a steady
course of efficient government, severity will very seldom be
found necessary, If, when punishment is inflicted, it is done
with composure and with solemnity, occasions for punishment will be very infrequent. Let a mother ever be affection-
ate and mild with her children. Let her sympathize with them
in their little sports. Let her gain the confidence by her assidu-
ous efforts to make them happy. And let her feel, when they
have done wrong, not irritated, but sad; and punish them in
sorrow, but not in anger.[16]

The idea of moving away from physical punishment toward affec-
tionate control probably seems like a good idea to most parents, but
what happens when it is not enough? It is well and good to explain
carefully the consequences of a bad behavior to your child, to induct him
patiently into your moral framework. But surely sometimes more is
needed.

Cora, aged twelve, lied repeatedly to her mother about doing her
homework. Even when her mother, Susan, received a personal note
from the vice-principal about the homework problem, Cora denied it
and said she had been mistaken for another girl. Cora's mother went
to the school and learned from the teachers that Cora's behavior in
class, except for the homework, was normal. The vice-principal suggested that Cora was at an age in which children often tested authority.

In this situation, all of Susan's well-reasoned pleas about the importance of being honest seemed to fall on deaf ears. A firm response was
needed. As with most lying incidents, there were two offenses, the
failure to complete the homework and the lie that followed. An appropriate punishment must distinguish between the crimes.

Most families have a set of escalating penalties for misbehavior,
which may include loss of TV or phone privileges or "grounding" (re-
striction to the home). These may work well enough, but they are
passive punishments, and usually unrelated to the crime. Active pun-

ishments related to the crime work better. For instance, if your older son repeatedly hit his younger brother, causing cuts and bruises, and then claimed he did not touch him, one method of punishment would be for the older son to do all the younger child's chores for a time. Part of punishment should be restitution to the victim, when there is one.

In Cora's case, Susan decided to supervise closely the nightly homework, and to take away TV privileges for one month. She believed that the TV was a major contributor to the problem. She told Cora that at the end of two weeks she would trust Cora to do her homework without standing guard. She let her know that, for her, lying about doing homework was worse than the unfinished homework. She said it was humiliating to play police officer, and she needed above all to feel that she could trust her daughter again. If Cora performed well, her TV privileges would be restored at the end of the month.

This punishment seemed to work with Cora, who realized there were definite limits on what her mother would tolerate. She also learned how strongly her mother felt about trust. Other punishments may have worked also. Punishments that don't work well are those that cannot be supervised and enforced, such as, "You may never watch TV again."

With many lies, there will be two punishments, one for the offense and one for the cover-up lie. The offender should understand that these are two separate punishments for two different offenses. The punishment for lying should reflect the consequences of the breakdown in trust. It would be appropriate to treat repeated lies about missed curfews with a few nights of house detention. The broken trust could be emphasized by insisting that the offender call home one or two times during the evening when privileges are restored.

Again, there is no punishment that is guaranteed, and as we have seen, there are great swings in attitudes about appropriate punishment. Here are some guidelines that reflect what scientists and therapists who deal with children's problems currently consider most effective:

- Avoid physical punishment.
- Separate the punishment for the lie from the punishment for the offense it is covering.
- In order to encourage the development of internalized moral precepts, emphasize the effect of the act on others, not just the evil of the act itself.
- Fit the punishment to suit the crime.

What does a parent do if, after weeks of talking about the problem and repeated punishments, his child still does not do his homework and continues to lie about it and perhaps other activities as well? In chapter 2 it was pointed out that there is indeed a strong correlation between chronic lying as a child (which often occurs with other bad behaviors) and adult criminal activity. This does not mean that your child will certainly become a criminal, but it is a serious warning to you as a parent that your child needs help from a professional counselor. Unfortunately, children's lies are not normally covered in medical training. Your pediatrician may not take it as seriously as you should. It is then up to you as a concerned parent to investigate the mental health profession to find a counselor who has experience and training in dealing with children who are chronic liars.

SPECIAL-CIRCUMSTANCE LIES: DIVORCE AND DAY CARE

As modern parents, we have inherited all of the child-raising difficulties experienced by our parents, and we have added some threatening new ones as well. As many as one half of our children will experience the divorce of their parents, and more than one half will surely spend a good part of their early childhood in day care situations.

These modern changes in our children's lives often generate in us a sense of anxiety and confusion, but provide no clear guidelines on how to act. Parents who have a difficult time coping with their children's lies in the best of circumstances often feel paralyzed when confronted with lies in these special circumstances.

Divorce

If the current rate of divorce continues, at least half of the children under eighteen will experience the divorce of their parents.[17] Divorce is a traumatic experience for parents and children. It can provoke aberrant behavior on the part of both the parents and children when emotional resources to deal with aberrance are completely drained. My own experiences as a family law practitioner and as a divorced parent have convinced me that it is a rare child whose moral development will be untouched by the experience.

PARENTS' LIES ABOUT DIVORCE

It is usually the parents who lie first in a family breakup. The divorce is often years in the making, and the symptoms are evident to the child. Yet the parents feel obliged to protect the children from truths they fear will upset the child's world. At the critical point of separation, most parents withhold critical information or simply lie to the children to get through the experience. In the most thorough study of the effect of divorce on children, *Surviving the Breakup*, a five-year follow-through of 60 families and 131 children, the authors, Judith S. Wallerstein and Joan Berlin Kelly, find that four fifths of the youngest children were not given an adequate explanation of the divorce or assurance of continued care. In effect, they woke up one morning to find one parent gone. The parents were usually so preoccupied with their own overwhelming problems that they could not deal with the needs of their children. Fewer than 10 percent received adult help from their community or family friends and fewer than 5 percent were counseled by a church congregation or minister.[18]

A student of mine, Marjorie, now twenty, told me about the breakup of her family ten years ago. "At dinner one night my mother told us that Daddy was on a business trip for a few weeks. This was very unusual because my father rarely traveled. We kept asking about him for several weeks, but my mom became angry every time we asked her. Finally we just stopped asking. We just never talked about Daddy again, even my brother and I together. It was as if it were some horrible secret that we couldn't talk about. I didn't see my dad again for three years."

KIDS' LIES FOLLOWING DIVORCE

The painful transition period following divorce is often one in which all the familiar structures of the child's life are rearranged or taken away. The house, the school, old friends, and most of all the identity of the child as part of a family with two parents disappear. During this period, the moral development of the child may be severely disrupted, and sometimes the child's behavior regresses with episodes of petty theft, cheating, and lying.

Lying for some children takes the protective strategy of fantasy. Wallerstein and Kelly reported that little girls very often had fantasies about their absent fathers, in which they became the center of attention. Wendy, age four, confided that she sees her father all the time (not true). He has an apartment but "he lives with me. He sleeps in my bed every night."[19]

If the behavior of parents is the greatest single determinant of the behavior of the children, many children of divorce must suffer the consequences of the lies and half-truths told to them during divorce. For a few, however, it may become a harsh lesson in favor of truth telling. Wallerstein and Kelly report a conversation with a fourteen-year-old girl, who offered, "Even though my mom and dad are dishonest and I used to be, I suddenly stopped lying. I don't know why, I just stopped lying last year. I decided that I didn't want to be like them and that I would tell the truth."[20]

Although parents cannot prevent the trauma of divorce for children, they can ease the anxiety by more forthright communication before, during, and following the divorce. Children need to know what is going on, and are made more anxious by sugar-coated explanations or by no explanation at all. Above all, parents must avoid lying to their children and jeopardizing the bond of trust, critical during these troubled times. Although parents don't have to reveal every detail of the trouble between them, they must let the children know what is happening and what their future arrangements will be. They must assure their children that rearrangement will not mean abandonment.

VISITATION AND KIDS' LIES

Many divorced families settle down into a fairly regular pattern of custody and visitation within a few months following the divorce. In my experience as a family law practitioner, the visitation pattern presents particular problems for raising a truthful child. Under the best of conditions the child's loyalties are divided, and his everyday life may be divided as well. With the popular (I believe unconsidered[21]) push toward joint custody, some children spend literally one half of the week with one parent, and one half with the other. Children in diapers shuttle between the two households on a perfectly divided timetable.

Even under the more traditional custody arrangements of established residence with one parent and visitation every other weekend and a couple of week nights, the child's world is divided. Different rules are imposed regarding junk food, pajama wearing, and all the details that make up a child's familiar environment. The child must become infinitely flexible, so as not to displease either parent.

In order to cope with his new bifurcated life and his divided loyalty, the child often constructs a distinct mental wall. It has been my experience, and that of friends and clients who have endured custody arrangements, that the child is more than reluctant to discuss anything that occurs in the household of the other parent.

The child's reluctance to divulge often runs directly against the parents' nearly obsessive need to know what is going on in the other household. Many parents, badly wounded from the divorce, insist on obtaining details about the ex-spouse's new romantic interests, about the restaurants where the child is taken, even about the furnishings and kitchen equipment of the former spouse's new residence. In addition, a parent's normal need to protect and control the child extends to the time the child is living in another household. The child is caught in a terrible bind. To reveal such details may seem a breach of loyalty to the child, not to reveal may anger or hurt the questioning parent. Many children handle this impossible situation by simply creating a fictional world.

One of my clients, let's call her Marge, reported angrily to me: "You can't imagine what is going on with John. Lisa told me that he lives in a beautiful apartment with a huge swimming pool and that he goes to fancy restaurants every night. Where is he getting the money? He claims he is broke!" When Marge learned that in fact John was living in a squalid apartment with no swimming pool, she was shaken. "Why would Lisa want to lie to me?" she asked in bewilderment.

Privacy is important to all children, but it is critical for a child who is trying to survive the delicate balancing act of living in two worlds, pleasing two separate parents. Fearing loss of control of the child, and consumed with a desire to know what is going on with the former spouse, a parent too often forgets the child's need for confidentiality.

The child's needs must come first. To avoid putting the child in a situation in which lies seem the only way out, a parent must develop a short "need to know" list. This list might include:

> If the child is sick while visiting the other parent
> If the child is physically or mentally abused

Beyond this, the parent can take the stance of a friendly nonjudgmental listener, if the child feels like talking. It will take enormous discipline on the part of the parent to suppress questions, but it is in the best interest of the child's mental and moral development.

SINGLE PARENTS AND KIDS' LIES

One of the consequences of divorce is that many children end up spending most of their life with a single parent. Ninety percent of the time this single parent is the mother. In addition to the fact that parenting often needs the energy of two adults, the single-parent mother is usually burdened by too much work and too little money. More than half of the time, families headed by women lose their struggle to remain above the poverty line.

A single-parent family can provide the same grounds for strong moral development as a two-parent family. Sometimes the experience of divorce brings parent and child closer together and offers the child a heightened sense of responsibility that could contribute to moral growth.

The potentially fatal flaw in the single-parent arrangement is the lack of time. A mother (or father) who is trying to do the work of two with little or no outside help is too often an exhausted parent who cannot provide the constant supervision and structure that children need. Dinner, which in the old days may have been a leisurely sit-down meal with time for talk, too often becomes fast food at a drive-in, or a TV dinner with the TV on.

In a massive study by Dornbush et al., scientists at the Stanford Center for the Study of Youth Development, 7,514 adolescents were carefully examined in terms of their family situations and their patterns of social deviance. As part of the examination, the scientists compared those living in mother-only households with two-parent households. They controlled for family income and parental education.

The researchers found that teenagers in mother-only households were more likely to exhibit deviant behavior than teenagers in two-parent households, and that boys exhibited more deviance than girls.[22] Lying is only one of the socially deviant acts that occurred more frequently in the mother-headed household; others included contacts with the law, school truancy, school discipline, and runaway activity.

The big difference between the two households was the pattern of family decision making. In single-parent families, boys, more often than girls, were far more likely to make decisions themselves, while in the two-parent family parents exerted more control in decision making.

Why should the mother-headed family make decisions differently? Although each family is different, it is easy to understand how the harried single mother could lose communication with and control of her teenage son. The areas of decision making investigated were choosing clothes, how to spend money, which friends to go out with, and how late to stay out. Obviously, all teenagers want more control of these decisions as they grow older and more independent, but in the mother-only families the male teenagers virtually took complete control at an early age.

Some single mothers feel physically incapable of controlling a growing boy. My friend Rhonda has been a single mother for ten years. She and Jason got along very well until he was fourteen. In that year Jason did not even bother to make up lies about missing his curfew; he simply said, "I am going to stay out late, and what can you do about it?" Rhonda felt helpless. She told me, "He is six inches taller and forty pounds heavier than me, how can I stop him?"

We may say that Rhonda does not have to rely upon physical superiority, there are other, more effective means of controlling children, but Rhonda does not feel that way.

An intriguing second observation is that when another adult was present in the single-parent household, the decision making became more like the two-parent family and deviance was reduced. This other adult could be a grandparent, lover, or friend, but not a child or stepparent.

The scientists did not venture to guess why the presence of an additional adult made a difference in the pattern of decision making. Perhaps the adult simply provided moral support for the mother or the incentive for a regular dinner hour. Or perhaps the other adult lightened the mother's chores and gave her more precious time.

STEPPARENTS

Nearly 75 percent of women, and a higher percentage of men, who divorce eventually remarry. One out of every six children in America today is a stepchild. These new families, variously called "blended," "merged," or "reconstituted" families, face special challenges. Our family is such a family. Tom is the child of my first marriage, and Eve, our eight-year-old, is our child. We are well aware of the everyday problems this imbalance creates.

For the moral development of the child, it is not clear that the advent of a stepparent is a blessing. In the Stanford Study for Youth Development noted above, the presence of a stepparent did *not* improve the rate of teenage male deviance over that of mother-headed families, while the presence of any other adult did. For female teenagers, it was a small improvement over mother-headed families.[23]

Children raised in stepfamilies have suffered all of the problems of divorce and now they must add new ones. Most of the children will still be visiting their other natural parent, so their lives are already divided. The timetable of visitation arrangements in a blended family can rival that of a major airline. The new stepfamily will, at least initially, struggle to blend two different life-styles. Therefore, the child must learn to live with three different family styles.

In the critical area of discipline, which strongly influences a child's moral development, the multiplicity of styles may be damaging. I overheard an eight-year-old friend of my daughter confide to her: "My mother grounds me, my stepfather yells, and my real father spanks." Even in an intact family disagreements about disciplinary styles can cause confusion, but the confusion is compounded in a stepfamily.

The best advice from those who study stepfamilies is to give the new relationships time to develop and to emphasize communication. In most instances, a child will be skeptical of the new arrangement. He will feel a new surge of loyalty to the natural parent who is left out of this family. It is foolhardy for the new stepparent to try to take over the role of the left-out parent. It will only cause resentment. On the other hand, it is impractical, if not impossible, to combine two families with two sets of rules. Frequent family councils where the children have a role in establishing new, mutually agreed upon rules is a good approach. And for a long while the natural parent should take the responsibility of discipline.

Not only do the rules change, but the whole cast of characters changes when families combine. Children who were the center of their single parent's world often feel they have become part of the crowd scene. They may be forced to share rooms with their old siblings, or their new stepsiblings. A whole new complex drama of sibling rivalry and alliances is suddenly thrust upon them.

It is not difficult to understand why this new family places a strain on the child's self-confidence, indeed on his very identity. Under these circumstances, children may indeed develop fantasy lies to shore up their sinking confidence.

Truthful, moral, confident children can develop in a "blended" family, but the parents must take special steps beyond those required in an original family. These should include:

- Insisting that the natural parent take charge of direction and discipline at least until new bonds have been firmly formed
- Holding frequent family councils with children's input into rule making and decisions
- Paying special attention to the needs of children who may feel displaced by new stepparent and/or new siblings

Some experts recommend family counseling as a necessary precaution for all blended families, even before trouble signs appear.

Day Care and Lying

The problem with day care and the development of a truthful, moral child is that the young child often spends more time in the company of other adults and children than he does with his own parents. If truthful children are taught by the example of truthful parents, and if styles of discipline influence the internalization of moral rules, how can parents control these factors when they are not present?

More than 50 percent of mothers with infants less than one year old have already returned to work. For most of these mothers, work is not a choice, it is a necessity. With the shift away from a manufacturing economy toward a service economy, the average wage in America *fell* by 13 percent between 1975 and 1983.[24] Day care is not a matter of personal preference for most families, it is a necessity of life.

The experts disagree about the effect of day care on children. But responding to the increased demand brought about by working mothers, the majority seem to nod favorably in its direction.

Even Dr. Spock, who had firmly advocated a full-time mother, changed his stance in his 1976 edition. He asserted: "Parents who know they need a career or a certain kind of work for fulfillment should not simply give it up for their children." He suggested that these parents "work out some kind of compromise between their two jobs and the needs of their children, usually with the help of other caregivers."[25]

But the experts premise their qualified support of day care on "good" day care. With our current national policy of insisting that day care is an individual solution, there are enormous variations in the availability of reasonably priced "good" day care. Excellent facilities may be available in Tempi, Arizona, while Dayton, Ohio, offers little.

As parents we must take the responsibility to find a day care arrangement in which we feel confident that our child will develop well, both emotionally and morally. This is never an easy task, since day care arrangements are often too few or too expensive, but it is an essential task.

Burton White, in his influential book *The First Three Years of Life*, believes that parents or grandparents are the best caretakers for infants and very young children. If the parents are forced to look for caretakers outside the family, however, he insists that this is a serious responsibility, which takes a great deal of investigation.

His recommendation for the best arrangement is, in order of preference:

1. Individual care in your home by a trained person
2. Individual care in the home of another person who is trained in childcare.
3. Family day care, which should involve a trained person with no more than two children under eighteen months or three children from eighteen to thirty-six months

4. A nonprofit day care center with the same ratio of caretakers to children as above and a supervisor with training in early childhood education
5. A day care center that is profit oriented, with the same considerations as the nonprofit center.[26]

To raise a moral child, parents should make sure the caretaker has similar ideas about discipline and is skilled in communication. Parents need to get a full report of the child's behavior, both good and bad. They need to trust the judgment of a caretaker to handle a behavior problem as they would.

Melissa, age four, came home from her new family day care and told her mother that Jason, also age four, was beating her up every day. Her mother reacted with concern and immediately confronted the day care mother with the problem. The day care mother, who had appeared thoroughly forthright and was very experienced, completely denied the allegation and claimed she never allowed the children to hit one another.

Who to believe? Georgia, Melissa's mother, like all working mothers, was extraordinarily dependent upon her day care mother, and she had spent many days searching for this one. On the other hand, she certainly couldn't expose her child to continuing brutality. In this instance, Georgia and the day care mother were able to discuss the problem. The day care mother agreed to watch the interaction between Melissa and the boy very carefully. At the end of the day, the day care mother reported to Georgia that the boy had not hit Melissa, but he had taken her toy twice and her potato chips at lunch and had tripped her at least once.

Melissa was not lying, she was calling for help. To her, the repeated small incidents of terrorism by a new child in a new place felt like being beaten. In this situation the mother could communicate with the caretaker and felt confident they shared the same values. She and the day care worker were able to work with the boy and his parents, and after a time the two children actually became friends.

Putting a small child into the care of another assaults our protective instincts as a parent. We immediately react with guilt and fear when we suspect our child is not being properly protected. It is not surprising that the very few incidents of sexual abuse in day care situations have blown up into a national paranoia about the dangers of day care. This is not to say that your child's allegations about wrongful touching or sexual abuse should not be taken seriously. (I will treat issues of lying and sexual abuse in the next chapter.) But we must keep in mind that most day care workers are dedicated adults who accept the very low pay and low status attached to their jobs because they love children.

At the height of one of the more lurid trials involving multiple allegations of sexual abuse in a day care setting, I came to pick up my daughter at her Montessori day care. Jan, her caretaker, a twenty-two-year-old Berkeley graduate who had taken off a year to work with kids, looked sad. When I asked her what was wrong, she said, "It's not fair! We work hard, we love our kids, and now the parents look at us suspiciously and we can't even hug our kids anymore!"

FINAL NOTE

Raising truthful, trustworthy children is probably a greater challenge today than it was for our parents. Yet this critical concern for all parents has received very little scientific study. We are forced to rely on prevailing expert opinion that seems to swing to meet cultural needs. The fast-changing expert advice on spanking and on the effects of day care are examples of this. The effect of divorce on the moral development of children has received little or no scientific study.

It seems unfortunate to me that the only area that has captured the attention of scientists is the credibility of children as witnesses, which I shall discuss in the next chapter. It is unfortunate because it takes lurid headlines about sensational issues to attract scientific attention. The garden-variety lies that we parents struggle with do not capture headlines or scientific attention.

CHAPTER SIX

Kids' Testimony in Court: The Sexual Abuse Crisis

by Mary Ann Mason Ekman

WHEN I WAS IN LAW SCHOOL NEARLY FIFTEEN YEARS AGO, IT was accepted wisdom that children make terrible witnesses. You could almost never consider testimony of a child under age seven, and above that age until about fourteen it was chancy. Children were called upon as witnesses only as a desperate last resort. To support the view that children were completely unreliable witnesses, the venerable research of the Belgian psychologist, Varondeck, was put forth. In 1891 Varondeck was called upon as an expert witness to defend an accused murderer. The only witness to the murder was an eight-year-old. Varondeck asked twenty eight-year-olds to identify the color of the beard of one of their teachers. Nineteen of the eight-year-olds obligingly responded with a color; only one student made the correct observation—that the teacher had no beard.[1]

In the past decade the attitude toward the child witness has dramatically reversed itself. Now children, sometimes younger than seven, appear in great numbers in family courts and criminal courts. Their testimony is often taken more seriously than similar testimony from an adult.

What has changed is not the degree of sophistication of modern children, but rather society's urgent need to protect children from what appears to be an epidemic of sexual abuse. Usually the child is the only witness, and there is no additional evidence. To refuse to allow the child to testify might jeopardize the protection of the child or spare from trial a person accused of a crime considered by many to be the most heinous. The public cannot tolerate this.

In 1975 about 12,000 incidents of child abuse were reported. By 1985 the number had passed 150,000. Public awareness of the growth of sexual abuse was inflamed by the grotesque revelations about massive abuse in day care centers from Florida to California.

Does this explosion accurately indicate a growth in offenses, or does it reflect a change in public attitudes about reporting? Or perhaps, as a nation have we been caught up in an hysteria about sexual abuse that prompts children to report abuse where none exists?

These are difficult questions to which we do not yet have the answers. In the light of our new awareness, there have been dramatic changes in the public schools and welfare and social assistance programs that deal with children. Through videotapes, storybooks, and presentations, children are encouraged to report sexual abuse to their teacher or parent. And in increasingly large numbers children do. Teachers, nurses, and mental health workers are often now legally required to report a "reasonable suspicion" of sexual abuse, where before they had no such obligation.

And accusations of sexual abuse by a parent are cropping up regularly in custody disputes. As an attorney who has practiced family law and researched custody issues, I am more than alarmed by this phenomenon. According to some judges, sexual abuse is alleged in 10 percent or more of all custody disputes that reach their court,[2] and the number of custody disputes has grown rapidly, pushed by the greater numbers of divorce and the radical changes in custody laws.

Critics of the sexual abuse statistics claim we have been caught up in a reporting hysteria. They allege that children, who they say are highly suggestible, have been encouraged to imagine behavior that didn't occur. Divorced mothers are singled out for special blame. They supposedly manipulate or brainwash the child in order to wrest custody from the father.

On the other hand, the vast majority of social workers and prosecutors working with children who claim they were abused continue to believe the children.

Overwhelmed by sexual abuse cases, federal and state courts have sought help from social scientists, mental health researchers, and constitutional experts. The courts hope to introduce reforms in the preparation of the witness and in courtroom procedures that will maximize the credibility of the child's testimony and protect the child while still preserving the constitutional rights of the defendant.

At the heart of this effort toward reform is a serious reexamination of children's credibility. We know already from the experiments with three-year-olds described in chapter 3 that even very young children are capable of telling outright lies. Different questions are: Can children be easily led into telling lies in order to please adults? Are children more suggestible than adults? Are they more likely than adults to believe their own lies? Do children manufacture their own fantasies to deal with stressful situations? Yet another question is: Are children capable of recalling the truth in sufficient detail to convict an offender? Using more sophisticated research methods and armed with a greater knowledge of child development than Varondeck had at hand, scientists are now probing the critical areas of suggestibility, memory and recall, understanding, and fantasy. Although there are still many questions to explore, the results of their findings will be examined later in this chapter.

There are important differences among sexual abuse cases, and therefore I shall deal with them separately. It is the mass abuse cases that have captured the public attention, and these present unique problems regarding the veracity of the children involved. Mass abuse cases, many of them centering around day care facilities, involve many victims and many defendants. Because of their complexity, they often drag on for years. By the time the child gets to court, if indeed he or she does, he or she may have been interviewed more than a dozen times.

Sexual abuse allegations against one parent in a custody dispute are a very different matter from criminal allegations. These are civil, not criminal, matters, and therefore the pretrial and trial procedures are entirely different. Although these cases rarely reach prime-time TV, they are growing in number.

And lastly, the great majority of cases involve the abuse of an individual child, often by a family member or close friend. These are the cases that are being reported in staggering numbers by teachers and other caretakers under the new reporting laws.

MASS ABUSE CASES

The most noteworthy fact about the many cases across the country that alleged the abuse of hundreds of children by scores of adults, usually in day care settings, is that very few alleged offenders are ultimately convicted. Most of the charges against most of the defendants are finally dropped. This has caused great public confusion. Are the prosecutors overzealous or have the children gone mad?

The public's introduction to the mass abuse world occurred in the spring of 1984 with the "Jordan sex case." America learned that in a small Minnesota town, which appeared to have all the wholesome virtues of the Midwest, two dozen men and women, most of them married, most of them solid citizens, were involved in a conspiracy to sexually abuse and sometimes torture their own children. Stories of parties where the parents competed to decide which parents would have sex with each other's children were related by the children. The children were taken from their homes and put in foster homes, and still the stories grew. Finally, the children began to talk of murder. Several children claimed they witnessed the torture and murder of one boy at one of the sex parties, and some mentioned the murder of other children as well.

Extensive investigations were begun to locate the bodies of the murdered children. The trials of the defendants began, and suddenly all charges were dropped by the attorney general's office.

What had gone wrong? In testifying against the defendants, the children began to admit they were making up the murder stories, although they did not recant on their account of the child abuse. At the same time, the original defendant, a two-time-convicted sex offender who had accepted a light sentence in return for his story, totally changed his story. He had backed the children's allegations and named multiple defendants. Now he said he acted alone.

It was clear that some of the children had lied about some of the events, and the prosecution did not believe it could convince a jury with such contradictory testimony. As in most mass abuse cases, extensive investigations of all the defendants' homes had not turned up a shred of corroborating evidence regarding abuse or child murder. The only corroborating evidence had been the account of the original defendant, now recanted, and indecisive medical evidence. Medical evidence regarding sexual abuse can be very ambiguous. Even when it is fairly clear cut, as with a ruptured rectum, it does not indicate who committed the offense.

Fingers of accusation were pointed all around, but most of them were aimed toward the now celebrated prosecutor, Kathleen Morris, who had begun the prosecution with great public furor, carried through the investigation in the limelight of the media, and then made the abrupt decision to drop the case. She was charged with bungling the whole case, from the amateurish investigations to the decision to go for all twenty-four defendants at once, rather than starting with the strongest case. She was called power-hungry, erratic, unprofessional.

Kathleen Morris became the scapegoat both for those who believed the children were telling the truth, and would now lose their day in court, and for those who believed the children were lying and had been encouraged in their stories by an ambitious prosecutor. But it appears to me that the same pattern that unfolded in Jordan, Minnesota, is evident in most massive child abuse cases. This pattern includes:

- A single incident quickly widens into an ever-larger circle of victims and defendants, often including some very unlikely defendants.
- Very convincing reports are given by even the youngest children on the details of the sexual abuse.
- No corroborating evidence other than medical evidence is given, some good medical evidence, most ambiguous.

- After a period of time following the original allegations, more bizarre stories are told by some of the children. These can include tales of satanic cults and child murder.
- Children's testimony contradicts itself on many details after much retelling. Children contradict each other.
- Prosecution tries to save "reliable witnesses," drops others, case falls apart.

The McMartin Preschool is the most celebrated, and at one point was the largest, mass abuse case. At the highest point of its investigation, 350 children out of 400 interviewed claimed they had been sexually abused by someone at Virginia McMartin's preschool in Manhattan Beach, California. Eventually 208 counts of child molestation and conspiracy were charged against 7 defendants, including the matriarch, seventy-seven-year-old Virginia McMartin, by 41 child witnesses.

Unlike small town Jordan, this case enjoyed the sophisticated resources of the Los Angeles Police Department Sex Abuse Unit. It also used a professional team of trained social workers from the Children's Institute to interview the children. In spite of these advantages, the McMartin case followed much the same pattern as the Jordan case.

The McMartin incident began with a single complaint by the mother of a two-year-old boy against Ray Buckey, the grandson of Virginia McMartin, the owner of the school. The investigation took fire rapidly, and soon the investigators went beyond the current student body and started interviewing students who had graduated in the past seven years. The 350 children who claimed they were sexually abused picked out at least three dozen suspects from the police photos, some of whom were friends of the McMartins, some civic leaders in Manhattan Beach.

As in the Jordan case, the police could find no corroborating evidence. The medical evidence of abuse (always controversial, since different medical examiners can reach different opinions) and the children's testimony, initially very convincing, were the only evidence.

As the interviews wore on, some of the older children began to tell tales of ritual abuse with black robes, black candles, and the drinking of animal blood. Several told of visits to local cemeteries, where they were forced to exhume bodies by Ray Buckey, who then hacked the bodies with knives.

It was at the pretrial hearing, which lasted for twenty months, the longest in California's history, that all the old fears about the reliability of child witnesses were realized. A pretrial hearing is not a trial with a jury, it is simply a step in the judicial process where the judge decides if there is enough evidence to send the defendant to trial. However, the defendant's lawyers are allowed to present an affirmative defense, and therefore the hearing can become a mini-trial without jury.

Forty-one witnesses were scheduled to testify against seven defendants, but it soon became evident that this could take months and months. The first witness, a seven-year-old, was cross-examined for a week. The second witness testified for sixteen days.

The attorneys for the seven defendants used three basic tactics to break down the children's testimony. The first tactic was to attack the interviewing procedures used by the therapists and the prosecutors. They used the videotaped interviews of the first interview to show that the interviewers were putting ideas of molestation into the children's heads. One therapist from the Children's Institute was shown, assisted by dolls and puppets, telling a child that the other children had already told them about the "crummy stuff" that happened at the preschool, adding, "I know you know what I am talking about." She told the boy that she and others wanted to find out who the "bad guys were," and asked for the child's help.[3]

The second tactic was to force the child into contradicting himself or the testimony of other children. With seven defense attorneys cross-examining the child's testimony for days on end, this was not difficult to accomplish with most of the witnesses. The defense attorneys were not always tough or tricky. Often they laughed with the witness and cajoled him into admitting a contradiction.

And finally the defense attorneys played up the children's testimony regarding ritualistic abuse or bizarre circumstances. The ninth witness claimed that the children at the school had been beaten regularly with a ten-foot bullwhip and taken to the Episcopal church, where they were slapped by a priest if they did not pray to three or four gods. Following his testimony, the embarrassed prosecutors decided to eliminate as witnesses all the other children who had mentioned satanic cults or rituals in the Episcopal churchyard.

As the child witnesses were systematically discredited on the stand or withheld for fear of damaging testimony about bizarre rituals, the case crumbled rapidly. At the end of the twenty-month hearing, the judge found that there was enough evidence to send all seven defendants to trial, but the prosecuting attorneys realized that, with the collapse of most of the children's testimony, they could never convict these seven defendants on the 208 counts charged.

In a publicly humiliating announcement, the prosecution team stated that they were dropping charges against five of the defendants and proceeding with a trial only against Ray Buckey and his mother, Peggy McMartin Buckey. Thirteen child witnesses, now between the ages of eight and twelve, would be testifying about events that occurred when when they were three, four, and five. At this writing the trial is still proceeding.

These two mass abuse cases illustrate the problems of obtaining convictions with child witnesses in general, and also the particular pitfalls presented by mass abuse cases.

Initial Interview

In all sexual abuse cases, whether there is one victim or four hundred, a critical issue is the initial interview. An interview that seems to encourage children to make allegations of sexual abuse is sure to make a jury question the credibility of the child. In the McMartin case, the videotapes of the original interview, which seemed strongly suggestive, were damning to the prosecution case. Repeated interviews over a period of months or years by different interviewers will almost certainly confuse the issue of veracity. I shall discuss later in this chapter the reforms that are being proposed to solve this problem area.

Trial Procedure

The second area of concern to all sexual abuse cases, both mass and individual, is the procedure of the trial itself. There is great concern about the child witness having to confront the accused offender face to face, a right guaranteed the defendant by the Sixth Amendment to the Constitution. During the course of the McMartin pretrial hearing, the California state legislature passed a law permitting the testimony of children on closed-circuit TV, where they could not see the defendant. Only the last witness was questioned under this new law. (The recent Supreme Court case, *Coy* v. *Iowa*, which will be discussed later, throws doubt on the constitutionality of this law.) There is also a strong feeling against using the same cross-examination tactics against children as are used against adult witnesses in criminal trials. Suggested reforms in these areas will also be discussed.

But mass abuse cases offer special problems not shared by other kinds of sex abuse cases. With multiple victims witnessing the same event, there is a far greater opportunity for contradictory testimony. Seven young children trying to recount the details of an event where a sex game was played, like the "Naked Movie Star" game described by many children at the McMartin pretrial, may well recall details of the event differently. An aggressive defense attorney can turn these contradictions into a circus of confusion. This kind of confusion is not limited to children. Many adults witnessing the same event will also produce contradictory testimony. This effect is enhanced if several years have passed since the event, as it often has with mass abuse cases.

And then there are the troubling reports by the children of bizarre rituals and satanic cults that have plagued most of the mass abuse cases. Both the Jordan case and the McMartin case foundered on these kinds of reports. In the Jordan case, the children who claimed they witnessed a child's murder actually admitted they had been lying. In the McMartin case, the prosecution withheld witnesses who they feared would ruin the credibility of their case with bizarre tales of graveyard rituals.

Children's reports of satanic rituals associated with sexual abuse have sprung up in virtually all parts of the country. According to John Crewdson, a journalist who investigated this phenomenon in his book *By Silence Betrayed*, there are striking similarities in the reports. The descriptions the children give of the rituals and chants are remarkably similar, and many report drinking a liquid that made them feel strange. Almost all describe ceremonial killings of small animals, and several mention the murder of other children, often babies. Police investigations of these reports have yielded nothing. They have excavated fields and drained ditches in search of bodies that are never found.[4]

In San Francisco, the police thought for a while they had a genuine satanic cult abuse connection. An alleged mass abuse case sprang up around a drop-in day care center on the U.S. Army's Presidio base. One of the small children allegedly abused talked of rituals with candles in a black room with crosses. Spontaneously, in the base grocery store, she pointed to a stranger and claimed he was one of the abusers. This stranger, Michael Aquino, was a major in the United States Army and also the self-proclaimed high priest of the Cult of Sed, an ancient Egyptian god. His wife, Letitia, was the high priestess.

The police, who had been following this purported cult's activities, were encouraged when the four-year-old girl was able to pick out the apartment house where the Aquinos lived, surrounded by ancient Egyptian statues and paraphernalia.

The case against the satanic high priest and priestess broke down rapidly, however, when no connection could be established between Aquino and the day care center or the other defendant, preschool teacher Gary Hambright. The description the little girl gave of the apartment where the rituals occurred did not match the decor of Aquino's apartment. Aquino, whose cultivated pointed eyebrows and pointed forehead hairline gave him a striking appearance, claimed in defense that children were always mistaking him for Mr. Spock or the devil. This case, like so many others, began to disintegrate, and eventually all charges were dropped.

Either there is a mass conspiracy of satanic cult pedophiles spread throughout the country, or there is a psychological explanation that has yet to be discovered. We know that nearly all very young children create fantasies. But usually these fantasies take on the form of a talking teddy bear, not the ritualistic murder of small animals or babies.

Bruno Bettelheim in his study of ancient fairy tales raises the issue of dark fantasy as an outlet for the child's anxiety about what he fears in the real world. In another work, *A Good Enough Parent*, he talks about the traditional role of holidays as providing psychological outlets for children. Halloween, he claims, symbolizes a child's persecutory fantasies:

> Before Halloween was bowdlerized, children were able to attain power for one night. To be able to dress and act like a witch, a devil, or ghost means that one shares by proxy in the secret power of these figures. Haunting adults was not done entirely in play: it was not merely the acting out of a wish to turn the tables on the adult world. It reached much deeper into the unconscious and satisfied a primitive need to identify with these primordial powers.[5]

Freud and Piaget, the twin giants of child development theory, have investigated children's fantasies, but they did not deal with dark fantasies. They did raise serious questions about children being able to separate fact from fantasy.

Freud did not claim that preschool-age children believe their fantasies are real, but he did suggest that their tendency to fantasize reduces their reliability. "The untrustworthiness of the assertions of children is due to the predominance of their imagination, just as the untrustworthiness of the assertions of grown-up people is due to the predominance of their prejudices."[6]

Piaget was more pessimistic than Freud. He believed that a child has difficulty separating fact and fantasy throughout his whole early childhood. "The child's mind is full of these 'ludistic' (pretend play) tendencies up to the age of 7–8, which means before that age it is extremely difficult for him to distinguish between fabulation and truth."[7]

Although some modern researchers have challenged Freud and Piaget, current research still shows that children are more prone to failures in distinguishing fact from fantasy than adults.[8] There is a debate about what kinds of fantasies are spontaneous, which seem to spring from the child's imagination, and which are influenced by actual situations. It may be argued that children are exposed to TV cartoons and comic books that foster bizarre fantasies.

We need more answers in the area of children's fantasies. We need to know about the content of children's fantasies as well as their ability to distinguish fantasy from fact. We need to pay particular attentions to those fantasies that dwell on ritual torture or satanic rites. Without these answers, many sex abuse cases will be dismissed by adults who believe that a child who talks about graveyards and devils must be lying about the central issue of molestation.

CHILD CUSTODY AND SEXUAL ABUSE

When a child in a custody dispute accuses a parent of molesting him, it arouses suspicion in the legal community that the other parent has brainwashed him into making this accusation. The problem with this suspicion, as with all prejudgments, is that it obscures the truth. Real incidents of sexual abuse are likely to be dismissed in these cases by critical judges. The problem is a serious one. The rate of accusations of sexual abuse has risen sharply over the past five years.

Those who take the position that allegations of abuse cannot be trusted point out that it is almost always the mother, not a social worker, teacher, or doctor, who initiates the charge against the father (the father, not the mother, is accused in the great majority of the cases). The mother may have a vindictive motive in trying to restrict the father's access to the child, or she may simply misinterpret what is going on with the father and child. A father alone with a child must now bathe

the child and change his diapers and may well touch the child in ways that he did not before. And, in fact, most allegations of sexual abuse in these cases involve fondling and exhibitionism, not penetration. The prestigious Family and Law program at the University of Michigan finds that more than half of the allegations of sexual abuse in custody cases are untrue.[9]

On the other side of the dispute are social workers and mental health professionals who claim that in many cases the abuse began before the divorce, but it is only after the breakup that the children feel able to speak up. They also point out that the stress of divorce and the loneliness of the parent can provoke abusive behavior, which may be seen by the abusive parent as a way of seeking love and solace. Many experts would agree with the findings of Richard Kruguman, director of the Kempe National Center for the Prevention and Treatment of Child Abuse and Neglect in Denver, whose study of sexual abuse allegations in eighteen custody disputes determined that fourteen of the charges were reliable, three were fictitious, and one was "too muddled" to sort out.[10]

We are in a custody crisis in this country. As a practitioner and writer on family law issues, I have observed drastic changes in the custody laws and in the nature of custody disputes over the past ten years. The rate of divorce has skyrocketed, encouraged by the nearly universal no-fault divorce laws, which not only made divorce easier, but helped promote a public acceptance of the event. Radical changes in custody laws followed the no-fault revolution. No longer is the mother always given the presumption of custody. Fathers are often awarded custody when they seek it, and there is a strong movement toward establishing joint custody. Over thirty states have passed laws that favor joint custody under some conditions, and in California the 1980 law gives first preference to joint custody. In California the court can impose joint custody even when it is opposed by one parent.[11]

There are more and more children each year experiencing the divorce of their parents and subjected to the confusing new custody laws. Very often parents are persuaded to accept, or the court imposes upon them, the modern preference for joint custody. According to Dr.

John Haynes, past president of the Academy of Family Mediation, "Within five years joint parenting will be the norm, even within the court system."[12] Yet very few divorced couples can cooperate on the elaborate arrangements it takes to split a child's life into equal halves. Friction builds up, and open hostility often follows.

Once joint custody is agreed upon, it is nearly impossible to get the order rescinded. Unfortunately, one of the only reasons for changing the order that the judge will consider is evidence of sexual abuse on the part of one parent. Sexual abuse is alleged so often that the American Academy of Child and Adolescent Psychiatry reported at its annual meeting in 1986 that the alarming increase in the number of sexual molestation cases was attributed to a greater public awareness of sexual abuse, laws requiring teachers and doctors to report even unsubstantiated accusations, careless counselors who interview purported victims with leading questions, and joint custody laws that in some cases lead mothers to fight harder for sole custody of their children.[13]

In dealing with the lives of children, our first duty is to protect them. It makes no sense to enforce joint custody agreements that are not in the best interests of the children. There is increasing evidence that joint custody is not a good solution for many of the families on whom it is imposed. At the 1987 Annual Meeting of the American Orthopsychiatric Association, a study was presented by the Center for Family in Transition about the effects of joint custody. Children whose parents had a relatively amicable divorce were not affected by joint custody, but those whose parents had a bitter divorce were psychologically worse off if the courts imposed joint custody than when they granted custody to one of the parents.[14]

In my opinion, joint custody agreements should not be preferred by the court, and should never be imposed upon reluctant parents. When they are agreed upon by the parents, they should be reviewable at the wish of either parent or the child. If the joint custody agreement is not working for either of the parents, it is not in the best interest of the child to enforce it. It is quite possible that this would reduce the number of allegations of sexual abuse that currently plague custody disputes.

But, at present, the court is forced to deal with increasing numbers of these accusations. The allegation of sexual abuse is a very different thing in a custody hearing than it is in a criminal trial. The defendant is not guaranteed his sixth-amendment rights to a jury or to be confronted with the witnesses against him. The judge can make a determination against the accused based on a "preponderance of the evidence," rather than the criminal standard of "beyond reasonable doubt."

Different states have widely different procedures for handling abuse accusations in custody cases. In many states, an allegation of sexual abuse is dealt with by Children's Protective Services, who investigate the claim and send it to juvenile court for a hearing if they determine there is sufficient evidence. In juvenile court the judge can deny access to the child for a period of time based on the preponderance of the evidence. This judgment will then be applied to the custody agreement in a later custody hearing. In some states the family court directly handles the allegation of sexual abuse.

In a family court or juvenile court the judge may well interview the child in his chambers rather than the courtroom. A child psychiatrist may also be called upon by the court for expert testimony, a testimony not often allowed in criminal trials. The expert is considered the child's advocate, not an expert witness for either parent. Each of the parents may bring in his or her own mental health expert as well.

This informality has both good and bad aspects. The bad aspect is that there may be little or no fact-finding by trained police investigators before the hearing, since this is not a criminal matter—the accused parent is not on trial.

The good aspect is that the child has usually not been forced to repeat his story many times before trial, and the trial itself may be less traumatic. If his testimony can be delivered informally out of sight of the accused parent, it is possible that his testimony may be more spontaneous and less guarded.

Unfortunately, judges in family law disputes are often totally untrained in dealing with allegations of sexual abuse. Yet they are forced to make quick decisions on an issue that not only gravely affects the life of the child, but the life and reputation of the accused parent as well.

When a judge calls in a child psychiatrist, he or she often relies heavily on that testimony. Some psychiatrists believe the judge encourages the psychiatrist to say whether or not a child is lying, and this is more than a psychiatrist can offer. According to child psychiatrist Melvin G. Goldzband, a well-known writer in the area of child custody and expert witnesses:

> The expert, for the most part, is simply not capable of making a flat statement regarding the absolute presence or absence of objective verifiable truth in the contestants' allegations. The psychiatrist can and ought to describe the character and personality structures of the individuals in question, and can state that lying may be more likely in certain types of character structures than in others (it is *possible* in all). However, in almost no case can the expert state flatly that the allegations made by one litigant about another are true or false.[15]

But many mental health professionals believe that they can quite accurately distinguish between a child who is lying about sexual abuse in a custody dispute from one who is telling the truth. Dr. Arthur Green, director of the Family Center at Presbyterian Hospital in New York, claims that there is a specific child abuse syndrome. He believes that, with few exceptions, a trained child psychiatrist can catch a child liar.

According to Green, when a child lies, he or she is often brainwashed by a vindictive or delusional mother who projects her own unconscious fantasies onto the spouse. In these cases, details of the sexual activity are obtained rather easily or may even be presented spontaneously by the child. The child shows little or no emotion in describing the abuse and often uses adult terminology. Genuine incest victims, on the other hand, claims Green, are secretive about their molestation. They often say nothing for weeks and sometimes retract and then restate their allegations. Their disclosure is usually accompanied by a depressed mood, and they describe the act in language appropriate for their age.

As an example of a false disclosure, Green tells the story of Andy B., brainwashed by a delusional mother:

> When Andy was seen alone with his father, he was friendly, spontaneous, and affectionate, and seemed to enjoy the interaction. When Andy was seen with both parents, he was angry and hostile toward his father. He humiliated Mr. B. by spontaneously drawing a picture of his father with a big erect penis, and told me that he and his daddy played with each other's penises while they were naked. During his narrative, which was presented without emotions, Andy's gaze frequently focused on his mother's approving expression.[16]

The California courts, which are often the pacesetters in introducing reform in procedures, have refused to allow expert testimony as to whether or not the child's behavior fits into the "sexual molest syndrome." They follow what is known as the Kelly Frye rule, which asserts that testimony based on a "new scientific process" is inadmissible without proof that it is generally accepted in the scientific community. In the case of three-year-old Sara, who was alleged by her grandparents to have been molested by her stepfather, the appellate court decided that the trial court should not have allowed a psychologist to testify that Sara showed signs of the "child molest syndrome," since this syndrome was not recognized by the American Psychological Association or any other professional organization.[17] Sara was sent back to live with the mother and stepfather.

But California courts have allowed mental health experts to relate the testimony of the child that would otherwise be considered hearsay (told by the victim to a third party), and not allowed as testimony against the abuser. In *The Matter of Cheryl H.*, the court allowed a psychologist to testify about what a three-year-old girl said about her father molesting her. This testimony was permitted as an exception to the hearsay rule, which allows statements not about the abuser but about the victim's state of mind. The court said:

> Although three-year-old sexual abuse victim's statements to the child psychiatrist that her father molested her were not admissible in dependency proceedings to prove that father actually abused her, evidence of victim's statements were admissible as circumstantial evidence that child believed father was the abuser, i.e., as circumstantial evidence of victim's state of mind.[18]

In sex abuse cases where there are rarely any eyewitnesses, this hearsay testimony is very powerful.

Clearly, the legal procedures must be reformed so that the judge is given clearer guidelines on how to make a decision. No parent should be allowed to use a false allegation of sexual abuse to withhold access to the other parent, but the child must always be protected.

First, the custody court or the juvenile court must have access to all the fact-finding and professional interviewing available in a criminal trial. An uninvestigated claim should not appear before the judge.

Second, there must be strict guidelines in the use of expert witnesses, who are usually mental health professionals. These experts are too often given the job of picking out a liar, which goes beyond the proven accuracy of the "child molest syndrome." Since there is often little or no additional evidence, this gives the expert more authority than is justified.

There is, in fact, a great deal of controversy about the use of psychologists and psychiatrists as expert witnesses in any court procedure. A recent study by Faust and Ziskin reported in *Science* claims that "considerable research shows that clinicians' judgmental accuracy does not surpass that of laypersons." For example, one study found that high school students could predict violent behavior in an individual just as well as mental health professionals.[19] This finding surely brings into question the ability of a mental health expert to accurately determine when a child is lying.

On the other hand, the purpose of a custody hearing is to protect the child, not convict a criminal. The looser interpretation of the hearsay rules to permit psychiatrists and psychologists to bring in evidence as to the child's state of mind may help to protect a child who cannot adequately speak for him or herself.

Third, although the rights of a criminal defendant are not in question, the accused parent deserves protection. The testimony of the accusing parent must be handled carefully. The court should not allow the accusing parent to report what the child said (hearsay evidence). The child himself must make this report. What about the very young child who cannot adequately testify? The court must then rely upon corroborating evidence, such as medical exams and the testimony of mental health professionals about what the child said in therapy. (Not whether or not the child is lying.) Since the judge does not have to hold a standard of "beyond reasonable doubt" in a civil case, the judge may well decide that the "preponderance of the evidence" warrants prohibiting the father (or mother) access to the child.

About half of our children will experience the divorce of their parents and the custody arrangements that follow. The conflict of loyalties and the tension between the parents may well provoke children to lie more frequently about many matters. In the last chapter I discussed the wall of privacy that a child creates between his two parents' worlds. Lying to one parent about the other world can occur. Trying to please a parent, a child may stretch the truth. On the other hand, a distressed parent may behave in a manner that he would normally consider unconscionable. Each case must be scrutinized with great care, and not dismissed as "another phony custody complaint."

REPORTING LAWS

The majority of child sexual abuse cases are not mass abuse cases or custody cases. They are usually incidents where an adult has noticed that the child is acting or talking strangely, or perhaps complaining about sore genitals. This person may be a parent or relative, but increasingly it is a teacher, school nurse, or child care worker. In most states the reporting laws that were established in the 1960s to require physicians to report "known cases" of abuse, both physical and sexual, were broadened in the 1980s to include therapists, teachers, and health professionals. California served as the model for many states, broadening the language of what must be reported from "known cases" to those in which there was a "reasonable suspicion."

Not surprisingly, the numbers of reported abuses steadily shot up in California following the expanded scope of duty to report. The reports overwhelmed the capabilities of the Children's Protective Services. The greatest increases came in physical, rather than sexual, abuse, because it was mandatory for a teacher to report suspicious bruises or signs of child beating. Evidence of sexual abuse is not so obvious, but reports of sexual abuse rose as well, from 9,120 in 1981 to 13,214 in 1983. During this period, sexual abuse education was instituted in many schools encouraging children to talk about matters that were previously forbidden.[20]

About 65 percent of the reports of child neglect and abuse have proven to be unfounded, according to Douglass Besharov, the first director of the U.S. National Center on Child Abuse and Neglect.[21] This arouses public suspicion that children are lying about being abused. Several thousand parents in thirty states have banded together in VOCAL (Victims of Child Abuse Laws) to protest that they were wrongly accused of child abuse and neglect.

But these unfounded reports do not necessarily mean that children are lying or that adults are lying. Hundreds of thousands of adults are required to report a "reasonable suspicion" of abuse, even when the child is silent. An unfounded report may also mean that there is not enough evidence to make a formal charge, not necessarily that abuse did not occur.

Mrs. J., a nursery school teacher, caught Jerry, age three, absorbed in a pornographic magazine he had apparently brought in his backpack. He pointed to a naked woman in a sexual pose and said, "That's Aunt

Ruth." Mrs. J. observed that Jerry, previously a popular boy, was now quiet and withdrawn from his playmates. She notified the Children's Protection Services. They contacted the parents and made a home visit. The parents were shocked and embarrassed. Aunt Ruth was a pretty young relative Jerry had met briefly and publicly at a family wedding. They agreed to take Jerry to a therapist, who found that Jerry was undergoing a normal, if somewhat exaggerated, developmental interest in sex.

Many states employ child abuse hot lines that will accept reports for investigation over the telephone even when the caller can give no reasons for suspecting the child's condition is due to the parent's behavior or when the caller insists on remaining anonymous.

The purpose of reporting laws is to protect children, and while it is better that we err on the side of overreporting, there are many who believe that the reporting system is out of control. Adults accused of abuse, who are most often parents, relatives, and friends, also have rights, and they may suffer irreparable damage to their reputations if they are the victims of a false report.

There are ways to make the reporting laws, and therefore the reporters, more responsible. Besharov suggests that first of all the laws must contain specific descriptions of what constitutes abuse, rather than the vague terms like "in danger" or "signs of abuse." For sexual abuse, behavior alone, without statements by the child or anyone else, is not sufficient to make a report. In the case of three-year-old Jerry, noted above, it certainly would have been wiser to choose another route, such as talking to the parents, rather than filing a complaint.

The second safeguard recommended by Besharov is to screen the complaints before a full investigation. The child abuse hot lines are barraged by reports that really reflect adolescent truancy, school problems, and sexual acting out, not real abuse.[22]

In the case of *Mammo* v. *Arizona*, the Child Protective Agency was successfully sued for not pursuing a complaint by a noncustodial father about a dangerous mother. The mother murdered her child. This decision has put fear in the hearts of screeners, but it is critical that a trained person separate the legitimate reports from those that are frivolous and reroute inappropriate calls to the appropriate social service.

USING A CHILD WITNESS WISELY

Greatly publicized cases like McMartin and Jordan have made the public wary about the credibility of child witnesses. The public has even been introduced to the confusing world of child abuse allegations in custody disputes. One of the nation's most popular TV shows, "L.A. Law," portrayed an incident in which a daughter was persuaded by her vengeful mother to falsely accuse her father of molesting her. On "L.A. Law," of course, the mother confessed and an agreement was reached.

In fact, the current researchers examining children's credibility as witnesses paint a more optimistic picture. The research indicates that even children as young as four can present reliable testimony. There are some caveats, however. The younger the child, the less detail they can recall. This is partly because the younger child cannot attend to as many details. It is also because the ability to comprehend, particularly new or unusual events, is not as developed. But when the event to be recalled is in familiar territory, like recalling the details of a cartoon presented for the first time, a child may recall more details than an adult.[23]

A major problem with the testimony of children under age ten is that the younger the child, the more difficult it is for them to recall freely. In order to tap their memory, the interviewer needs to guide the recall process.[24] This leads into the dangerous waters of suggestibility.

Suggestibility refers to the extent to which a witness can be led to believe details about an event that did not actually occur. In a legal procedure, the concern is that repeated interviewers will suggest new information that the witness then comes to believe is part of his actual memory.

Suggestibility is by no means a problem for children only. I was a subject in a demonstration given by one of the foremost researchers in the area of suggestibility, Elizabeth Loftus. A film was shown in which a red car is driven down a quiet street ending with a crash with another vehicle. In the questioning that followed, I was asked the location of the stop sign, when in fact it was a yield sign. I confidently reported the location, and later in the questioning I responded that I had seen a stop sign. So did the majority of the audience.

The issue then is not whether children are vulnerable to misinformation, but how much more vulnerable are they than adults? There is a great deal of ongoing research in this area, with some conflicting results. Generally, it is agreed that by the age of ten or eleven children are no more vulnerable than adults to misleading or incorrect information. There is controversy about children between six and ten years old. Some research indicates that they are no more susceptible to accepting misinformation than adults, and other research finds they are. With children under seven, the research indicates that they are particularly vulnerable to misinformation about peripheral facts, but not about the main event. Preschoolers are also very influenced by the adult questioning them.[25]

When Varondeck asked the children to describe the color of their teacher's beard, when in fact he had no beard, the children probably responded with a color to please the questioner. Many experiments have been done in which the interviewer provides misinformation about an event after a child has witnessed it. A clear pattern of suggestibility evolves. Children are most susceptible to misinformation if their original memory of the area of misinformation is weak; the misinformation deals with a peripheral, not central, event; and the interviewer who provides the misinformation is an adult they respect. In one experiment, when the misinformation was provided by a child rather than an adult, it was accepted half as often.[26]

The critical arena of suggestibility begins with the initial interview. The interviewer may be a social worker or a police officer with little or no training. Even those who are supposedly well trained may mislead a child. A standard interviewing technique is to give the child two anatomically correct dolls and ask the child to show what happened. Several studies have questioned what is really going on. One study compared twenty-five abused with twenty-five nonabused children and found that the differences between them were not that strong. In another study of one hundred nonabused children, nearly 50 percent interacted with the dolls in a manner that some interviewers could interpret as evidence of sexual abuse.[27] The prominent genitalia and orifices on the dolls possibly suggest a play pattern for young children.

Clearly, more research and development needs to be put into the crucial area of developing nonsuggestive techniques that are taught to all interviewers. King and Yuille, experts in the area of children's suggestibility, recommend doing away with dolls but adding several techniques based on what we know about children's development. One possibility is to use prompts, small-scale models of rooms and furnishings that can be moved around to help children remember; another is to practice tasks like photo identification so that a child can better understand the concept. Although young children may still require verbal prompts to promote recall, the information the interviewer must communicate to the child is that they do not have to remember everything; it is okay to say, "I don't remember."[28]

If children, even young children, can adequately relate a past incident if questioned properly, is it necessary for a judge to rule on their competency? Since the eighteenth century it has been well established that the judge in each individual case must determine through questioning whether the child demonstrated adequate veracity, intelligence, memory, and verbal capacity. Judges asked questions like: "Do you know the difference between right and wrong?" "Do you know the meaning of an oath?" Depending on the child's age, the judge may also ask the child to recite the alphabet, or recount addresses and phone numbers or teachers' names.

Pressed by the swelling numbers of sexual abuse cases in which the child is the only witness, there is a trend toward eliminating the competency examination and allowing a child to testify as any other witness. (Eight states so far have eliminated the requirement.) The jury, or judge, must decide if the testimony is believable. But whether a jury can adequately assess the competency of a child witness has not been adequately researched. Surely the jury needs some clear instruction on how to deal with children's testimony.

There is also a movement to stretch the hearsay rules, or to create a new hearsay exception for the sexually abused child. The purpose of the laws excluding hearsay statements is that out-of-court statements are by their very nature unreliable. Only when the statements are made in court, under oath, where the defendant can cross-examine them, are they considered reliable. In cases of sexual abuse, hearsay statements may be the *only* evidence if the child is found incompetent to testify. The three most common ways that hearsay is allowed into the court are if the child makes a medical complaint, if the child specifically complains of rape, or if the child makes an excited utterance. Traditionally, an excited utterance is made at the time of the event—i.e., "That man just put his hand under my dress!" But courts have been very lenient in sex abuse cases, admitting "excited utterances" that occur days, weeks, or even months later. Some states have even enacted a special sexual abuse exception to the hearsay rule in which another witness can introduce the child's statement if there is corroborating evidence.[29] These stretchings of the hearsay rules have not yet been tested by the Supreme Court.

There is yet another movement to protect the child from seeing the defendant in criminal trials. It is believed by those wishing to change the procedures that the child will be so unnerved that his testimony will be affected. Aside from that, they consider it cruel and possibly traumatic for a child to face his abuser. Some states have introduced closed-circuit television, with the defendant watching in a different room. Other states allow videotaped testimony in place of the live child witness in order to avoid the confrontation between child and abuser. Some states have decided that the child does not have to testify at all, and adult witnesses can relate what the child said about the event. This creates an exception to the usual hearsay rule that only an eyewitness can relate the story.

The U.S. Supreme Court, in *Coy* v. *Iowa* (June 1988), raised serious doubts about the constitutionality of these efforts to prevent the child from looking at the accused abuser. In this case, two thirteen-year-old girls were sexually assaulted while camping out in their backyard. The accused, John Avery Coy, was a next-door neighbor. An Iowa law designed to protect the victims of sexual abuse permitted the use of a screen between the accused and the girls that blocked him from their sight but allowed him to see them dimly and to hear them.

In the majority opinion, Justice Scalia strongly affirms the "right to confrontation" put forward by the Sixth Amendment. He asserts that the basis of this right is that it is more difficult for an accuser to lie when confronted by the accused and claims ". . . there is something deep in human nature that regards face-to-face confrontation between accused and accuser as 'essential to a fair trial in a criminal prosecution.' "[30]

In a concurring opinion, however, Justice O'Connor agrees that the Iowa law does not allow for confrontation, but insists that with many of the other new procedures in other states, including videotaped testimony in court, the testimony is made in the presence of the defendant. She also argues that there is still room for a law that treats the issue of confrontation on a case-by-case approach. "But if a court makes a case-specific finding of necessity, as is required by a number of states' statutes, . . . our cases suggest that the strictures of the Confrontation Clause may give way to the compelling state interest of protecting child witnesses."[31] This important Supreme Court decision leaves the new laws passed by many states in a state of limbo. Most likely they will each have to be reviewed and possibly rewritten to assure that they meet the test of this rather confusing decision.

In my opinion, the Supreme Court was correct both legally and morally in saying that we cannot easily give away constitutional rights. Public sympathy is surely with the possible suffering and discomfort that may be endured by a child in this situation, but in many ways it is the very situation for which the Sixth Amendment was adopted. In a crime where the word of the accuser is often the only evidence, the defendant has every right to protection from false accusations.

Douglass Tarrant, forty-one, assistant superintendent for finance of Pinellas County Schools in St. Petersburg, Florida, committed suicide before learning that the fifteen-year-old girl who had accused him of lewd and lascivious acts had recanted her story two days earlier.[32] Tarrant's case is not unique. Hundreds of members of the organization VOCAL claim they have been falsely accused. A false accusation of sexual abuse can ruin the life and reputation of an innocent victim more predictably than a false accusation of almost any other kind of crime.

Moreover, a leading researcher on this subject, Gary Melton, claims that the need for these reforms is undocumented and unstudied. We do not know for certain that a child will give better testimony if the defendant is not there, and we have no real evidence that confronting the defendant is always traumatic for every child. In fact, he suggests, for some victims it may be cathartic to finally face the offender and feel that a wrong may be righted.[33]

There are other procedures that do not challenge the Constitution that will make the child witness more comfortable. A child can be better prepared for what he or she can expect in the courtroom. Introducing the child to the courtroom and telling him or her about the cast of characters in advance can help the process. Once the child is on the witness stand, the attorneys can use simple direct questions, using the child's own vocabulary, to draw out the testimony. For instance, the attorney must learn what the child calls the sexual organs. The judge can control the cross-examination, controlling harassment and attempts to confuse the witness.

In civil trials to determine custody, or to secure an order to protect the child from an offending adult, there are no constitutional restraints, since there is no criminal defendant. Judges can informally question the child in their chambers if they wish, with the attorneys present.

Another important issue relates to the use of the testimony of expert mental health professionals who have examined the victim. This testimony is allowed far more frequently in civil cases than in criminal cases, since it is considered too prejudicial to the defendant. There are two kinds of information that these experts provide: by testifying as to the state of mind of the victim, they can provide details of an event that the child may not adequately explain in court; and by analyzing the behavior of the child, they may indicate if the child is really the victim of sexual abuse.

In my opinion, the exclusion of expert testimony as to the credibility of the child or to the child's state of mind makes sense in criminal trials. A criminal defendant is entitled to protection from what are still considered controversial observations on the part of the mental health professional, and from the secondhand testimony about what actually occurred.

A civil trial, where the object of the trial is to protect the child from a parent or guardian, is a different matter. The judge (there is no jury), should get all the information possible to protect the child. Experts should be allowed to testify as to the child's state of mind, and to their psychological makeup. However, at this time, testimony as to whether or not the child shows evidence of a sexual abuse syndrome is probably inappropriate, since this "syndrome" is not widely accepted.

THE FUTURE

When we are in the middle of a crisis, it is difficult to see down the road. The sexual abuse of children is surely a crisis, not just for the legal system and the Children's Protective Services, but for all parents who fear that the growing swell of reported abuse might somehow touch their children.

At the moment we have more questions than we have answers. But here are some of the things that researchers have learned:

- Children sometimes do lie about sexual abuse. This is more likely to occur in custody disputes, where they are influenced by one parent against another, or in mass abuse cases, where the process can encourage bizarre fantasies.
- If properly questioned, even very young children have good recall, but with less detail than adults. Young children are vulnerable to suggestions by adults.
- The new reporting laws do provoke a high rate of unfounded reports. However, they also reveal some incidents of abuse that would not have been uncovered previously.

Here is what we don't yet know, but researchers are continuing to study:

- How to conduct the critical initial interview. Are anatomically detailed dolls suggestive? How can a child be prompted without influencing his or her answers?
- What role fantasy plays in the recall of a child.
- Is a child traumatized by the sight of his or her abuser in court? Will this encounter restrict his or her testimony?
- How do juries react to the testimony of young children? Can they properly assess a child's competency?
- What is the proper role of mental health expert testimony? Can they really identify a sexual abuse syndrome?

The answers to these questions will help the courts strike the difficult balance between protecting the child victims of sexual abuse while still protecting the rights of the accused. These answers will also affect the use of child witnesses in other cases. But it is in the cases in which the child is both the victim and the only witness that the need is critical.

EPILOGUE

IT IS HARD NOT TO FEEL BETRAYED WHEN WE DISCOVER OR suspect that our child lied to us. It seems as if our child has turned against us. It does not seem fair. Our kid's lie blocks us from doing what we think we should be doing as parents. If we don't know what is happening, we can't intervene, protect, caution, advise, or punish (if that is what is called for).

Our child's lie asserts a change in who is in charge. Not us any longer, or so completely. Gone are the days when we could or should know everything. Now we must live with some uncertainty, now we must win our child's confidence or trust. When our child reaches the age when he or she can lie without always or usually getting caught, our child for the first time has a choice about what to share with us.

Whether our children will lie to us no longer depends upon how scared they are of being caught. They have learned they can get away with it. Now truthfulness depends, in part at least, upon how we have been and are as parents. How understanding or impatient, how trusting or suspicious, how fair or harsh we have been. Have we been so permissive or so preoccupied with our own lives and careers that we have been inattentive? Do they know we care what they do and how they act? How much has our child learned about why truthfulness is important? How well have we ourselves demonstrated truthfulness? How much effort have we expended to teach our children moral values?

Discovering that our child has lied, and nearly got away with it, confronts us with a loss of our own power. No longer can we be certain of having all the information we want. No adult has that with anyone else, but we do with our children, for a time. We must have that information, we must know how our children are feeling, what they want and need and plan to do when they are very young, for they totally depend upon us for their survival. But as the child grows, we no longer are their center, their only source, their only means for survival.

The lie asserts the child's right. The right to challenge us. The right to privacy. The right to decide what will and won't be revealed.

There is no question that parents need to know a lot about what their children are doing and planning. And that need does not end when the child becomes able to deceive us, it only becomes more difficult for us to be certain we can fill it.

Lying about serious matters is not a problem just because it makes it more difficult for parents to do their job. Lying erodes closeness and intimacy. Lying breeds distrust, it betrays trust. Lying implies a disregard for the person deceived. It can become nearly impossible to live with someone who lies often.

Lying usually accompanies other misdeeds, breaking other rules. When it becomes chronic, lying may be a sign of serious trouble, of disturbance in the child and in the family. If not dealt with, frequent lying may lead to serious problems in adulthood.

What are we to do when we suspect our child is lying? I, my wife, and my son, Tom, have given many specific suggestions. The most important thing is to try not to respond with anger, the anger born from feeling hurt, betrayed, or challenged. Try to understand why the lie is occurring, the motive for lying. Very often that understanding will allow you to talk to your child in a way that will allow the child to be truthful, which will eliminate the child's motive for lying.

It may require no more than acknowledging some misdeed your child has done. Try, as difficult as it may seem, to see the world from your child's view. Be on your child's side. Show forgiveness. Remember what it was like when you were a child. This doesn't mean giving up your rules or standards, but it does mean understanding rather than always punishing any infraction. And, as your child grows older, it means being willing to discuss or negotiate the rules you live by as a family.

Such understanding does not mean you won't sometimes also be angry about what your child has done. Children sometimes do very bad things that disappoint and anger us, and it is important that they know that. But even when a child has done something terrible, such as hurting another child or stealing, the parent's disapproval can be mixed with compassion. A road back to self-respect must be allowed, humiliation avoided. A terrible act, a desperate lie to conceal it, needs to be punished, but it also needs to be forgiven.

Sometimes parents suspect lying even though the child is being truthful. When a truthful child is disbelieved, the damage can be severe.

I was not more than thirteen when this happened to me. My mother would not believe me about an incident with a girl I was dating. The memory is still quite vivid. I was going steady with Mary Lou. In those days, in that small New Jersey suburb, that's what kids did at that age, for at least a few weeks at a time. One weekend night, which Mary Lou had told me she had to spend with her parents, I went to the movies and discovered her necking with another fellow two rows in front of me.

The next day I confronted her, called her a two-timer, asked her to give me back my class ring, and tore up her picture, which I had carried in my wallet, throwing the pieces at her feet. When I returned home my mother was furious, having heard from Mary Lou's mother that I had called her daughter a whore. I knew the word, but I had not used it. "Two-timer" seemed much more accurate, for Mary Lou was not betraying me with the entire classroom of boys! I was accused of lying.

The next day at school, Mary Lou denied that she told her mother I called her a whore, but she would not talk to her mother or mine. I never convinced my own mother of my innocence. I was grounded for two months and became very bitter. My mother died a year later. There never was an opportunity to clear the matter up.

When parents encounter such situations in which there is no way to find out the truth, they have a choice about which kind of mistake they want to risk. If they are trusting and accept their child's word, they risk being exploited and deceived if they were wrong. If they are suspicious and distrusting, they risk disbelieving a truthful child if they were wrong, and that I believe is more damaging. Our child then can no longer count on us, and that loss can be severe. The anger it breeds in the child may motivate the lies the suspicious parent had hoped to avoid.

Trust is intertwined with lying in many different ways. The lying child betrays the parents' trust. The parent who has been lied to must struggle to forgive the child and allow for trust to be reestablished. The distrustful parent may destroy the truthful child's belief in the parent's fairness and commitment. It may be useful to think that sometimes children lie to us because they don't trust us, they are not certain that they can be truthful to us without being hassled or punished.

Parents should not give up their beliefs in what is right, but they must also treat their children in a way that lets them know they can be trusted with the truth. Parents start with the child's trust, but as the child grows older, they must earn it.

APPENDIX

METHODOLOGICAL NOTES ON THE HARTSHORNE AND MAY STUDY

I have relied on many of the findings from Hartshorne and May's study, and while many of their findings have been borne out by subsequent scientific studies, some scientists have criticized their work.

One reason why their findings had so little impact is they emphasized the importance of situational factors. Their findings, according to the interpretation of many, showed that cheating is not related to a child's characteristics but depends on the particulars of each temptation. Recent reanalysis of their data suggests this is an overstatement. There are some consistencies, and it is possible to explain cheating to some extent by factors not due to the specifics of each temptation. The portion of Hartshorne and May's data I have focused on—the comparison between those who never cheated and those who cheated and then lied about it—emphasizes how these two groups of children differ.

Some scientists have worried that Drs. Hartshorne and May may actually have encouraged the children to cheat by making it so easy. Some kids see it this way. In my own research, some of the children who admitted cheating told me they didn't think it was wrong if the teacher isn't strict. Some teachers are so lax, they said, that they must not really care. This may just be rationalization. Studies in the last twenty years found more cheating in college classrooms, which rely on proctors and monitors, than in those classrooms that rely on the honor system.

Some critics think Hartshorne and May erred by having someone other than the teacher give the tests. Kids may be more willing to cheat if the person being cheated isn't someone they know, such as a school authority. By the same token, some people don't feel bad about cheating a large department store, but wouldn't cheat the proprietor of a mom-and-pop grocery. I don't think this criticism is very serious. The children were told these were tests. They were given in school, during class time. The tests were not identified as a research study. There is every reason, I would think, for the kids to take the tests seriously. Perhaps fewer kids would have cheated if the tests were given by the teacher, but our interest was not so much in how many cheated, but what distinguishes the kids who cheated from the ones who didn't.

Some scientists have objected to Hartshorne and May's study because the various opportunities to cheat or lie were not part of the child's life, but were introduced by the scientists. I think that criticism is unwarranted as well, for Hartshorne and May took care to set up situations that were similar to ones the child encountered daily.

NOTES

CHAPTER ONE

1. See John Phelan, *Scandals, Scamps and Scoundrels* (New York: Random House, 1982); also, Agness Hankiss, "Games Con Men Play," *Journal of Communication* 3 (1980): 104–12.

2. *Time,* July 18th, 1986, p. 68.

3. See Sissela Bok, *Lying: Moral Choice in Public and Private Life* (New York: Pantheon, 1978), chap. 3, for a discussion of these issues.

4. Svenn Lindskold and Pamela S. Walters, "Categories for Acceptability of Lies," *The Journal of Social Psychology* 120 (1983): 129–36.

5. These figures come from B. B. Houser, "Student Cheating and Attitude: A Function of Classroom Control Technique," *Contemporary Educational Psychology* 7 (1982): 113–23.

6. These figures come from Claudia H. Deutsch, "Students Cheating Even More," *New York Times,* repr. in *San Francisco Chronicle,* 15 April 1988, p. B3.

7. Prof. Gary T. Marx, "When a Child Informs on Parents," *New York Times,* 29 August 1986, p. 27.

8. *San Francisco Chronicle,* 12 September 1986, p. 1a.

9. *New York Times,* 22 August 1986, p. 8.

10. For clarity I have left out a few of the details, such as the fact that both boys and girls were studied. The full report appears under the title "Situational Influence on Moral Justice: A Study of 'Finking,'" by H. Harari and J. W. McDavid, in *Journal of Personality and Social Psychology* 11 (1969), no. 3: 240–44.

CHAPTER TWO

1. The full report—*Studies in the Nature of Character* (New York: Macmillan, 1928), vol. 1., *Studies in Deceit*—includes all this information.

2. See M. Rutter, J. Tizard, and K. Whitmore, eds., *Education, Health and Behavior* (New York: Wiley, 1970); M. K. Shepherd, B. Oppenheim, and S. Mitchell, *Childhood Behavior and Mental Health* (New York: Grune & Stratton, 1971); but not J. W. McFarlane, L. Allen, and M. P. Honzik, *A Developmental Study of the Behavior Problems of Normal Children Between Twenty-one Months and Fourteen Years* (Berkeley: University of California Press, 1962).

3. The quote is from "Honesty and Dishonesty" by Roger V. Burton, a chapter in Thomas Lickona, ed., *Moral Development and Behavior* (New York: Holt, Rinehart and Winston, 1976).

4. This study was reported by Charles D. Johnson and John Gormly in an article entitled "Academic Cheating," *Developmental Psychology* 6 (1972): 320–25.

5. Magda Stouthamer-Loeber mentioned this possibility in her article "Lying as a Problem Behavior in Children: A Review," which appeared in *Clinical Psychology Review* 6 (1986): 267–89.

6. Thomas M. Achenbach and Craig S. Edelbrock, "Behavioral Problems and Competencies Reported by Parents of Normal and Disturbed Children Aged Four Through Sixteen," *Monographs of the Society for Research in Child Development* 46 (1981), no. 188: also, by the same authors, "The Child Behavior Profile: II," *Journal of Consulting and Clinical Psychology* 47 (1978): 223–33.

7. Stouthamer-Loeber, "Lying as a Problem Behavior."

8. Richard Christie and Florence L. Geis, *Studies in Machiavellianism* (New York: Academic Press, 1970), p. 1.

9. Michael Korda, *Power!* (New York: Random House, 1975), p. 4.

10. Ibid., p. 327.

11. Dorothea D. Braginsky, "Machiavellianism and Manipulative Interpersonal Behavior in Children," *Journal of Experimental Social Psychology* 6 (1970): 77–99. A different version of the Mach scale was used in this study than the one I quoted.

12. S. Nachamie, "Machiavellianism in Children: The Children's Mach Scale and the Bluffing Game," Ph.D. dissertation, Columbia University, 1969. An abstract is in R. Christie and F. L. Geis, *Studies in Machiavellianism,* p. 326.

13. Christie and Geis, *Studies in Machiavellianism,* p. 332.

14. D. D. Braginsky, "Parent-Child Correlates of Machiavellianism and Manipulative Behavior," *Psychological Report* 27 (1970): 927–32, reported the inverse relationship between parents and children's Mach score. R. E. Kraut and J. D. Price, "Machiavellianism in Parents and Their Children," *Journal of Personality and Social Psychology* 33 (1976): 782–86, found a positive relationship.

15. Kraut and Price, "Machiavellianism"; M. Lewis, "How Parental Attitudes Affect the Problems of Lying in Children," *Smith College Studies in Social Work* 1 (1931): 403–404.

16. *Time,* 18 July 1986, p. 68.

17. M. Stouthamer-Loeber and R. Loeber, "Boys Who Lie," *Journal of Abnormal Child Psychology* 14 (1986): 551–64.

18. S. Dornbush et al., "Single Parents, Extended Households and the Control of Adolesecents," *Child Development* 56 (1985): 326–41. Also, L. Steinberg, "Single Parents, Stepparents, and the Susceptibility of Adolescents to Antisocial Peer Pressure," *Child Development* 58 (1987): 269–75.

19. Hartshorne and May, *Studies in Deceit,* bk 1, "General Methods and Results," p. 274.

20. D. Sherill et al., "Seating Aggregation as an Index of Contagion," *Educational Psychological Measurements* 30 (1970): 663–68.

21. U. Bronfenbrenner, "Response to Pressure from Peers Versus Adults Among Soviet and American School Children," *International Journal of Psychology* 2 (1967): 199–207 (quote from p. 201).

22. As discussed by Thomas J. Berndt, "Developmental Changes in Conformity to Peers and Parents," *Developmental Psychology* 15 (1979): 608–16.

23. Their article is entitled "Conformity to Peer-Sponsored Misconduct at Four Grade Levels," *Developmental Psychology* 12 (1976): 226–36 (quote from p. 235).

24. T. J. Berndt, "Developmental Changes in Conformity to Peers and Parents," *Developmental Psychology* 15 (1979): 608–16 (quote from p. 615).

25. Ibid., p. 616.

26. Charles M. Bonjean and Reece McGee, "Scholastic Dishonesty Among Undergraduates in Differing Systems of Social Control," *Sociology of Education* 38 (1965): 127–37.

27. To be more exact, on each of the thirty-seven questionnaire items, a child could earn a point if his rating was different from 90 percent of the other boys his age. The boys who accumulated the most points—the 10 percent who were most deviant from the rest—were followed up. The full study was reported in 1981 in the *Journal of Child Psychology and Psychiatry* 22: 19–33.

28. Hartshorne and May, *Studies in Deceit,* p. 377.

CHAPTER THREE

1. Stephen Ceci, personal communication, March 11, 1986.

2. Michael Lewis, Catherine Stanger, and Margaret Sullivan, "Deception in Three Year Olds," unpublished manuscript, n.d. The authors are at the Institute for the Study of Child Development, University of Medicine and Dentistry of New Jersey.

3. This study, "Lying and Misrepresentation of Reality in Four-Year-Olds" (draft ms.), is by Magda Stouthamer-Loeber, Linette Postell, and Rolf Loeber.

4. Most of the evidence against lying in young children comes from Jean Piaget, *The Moral Judgment of the Child* (Glencoe, Ill.: The Free Press, 1965; originally published 1932).

5. Heinz Wimmer, Silvia Gruber, and Josef Perner, "Young Children's Conception of Lying: Lexical Realism—Moral Subjectivism," *Journal of Experimental Child Psychology* 37 (1984): 1–30.

6. C. Stern and W. Stern, *Monographien uber die seelische Entwicklung des Kindes. s. Brand: Erinnerung. Aussage und Luge in der ersten Kindheit* (Leipzig: Barth, 1931; originally published 1909), 4th ed. (as quoted by Wimmer, Gruber, and Perner, "Young Children's Conception of Lying," p. 28).

7. Eugenie Andruss Leonard, "A Parents' Study of Children's Lies," *The Pedagogical Seminary* 27, no. 2 (June 1920), p. 130.

8. C. C. Peterson, J. L. Peterson, and D. Seeto, "Developmental Changes in Ideas About Lying," *Child Development* 54 (1983): 1529–35.

9. This quote is from a thesis on lying in children by Marie E. Vasek, "Lying: The Development of Children's Understanding of Deception," Master's thesis, Clark University, Worcester, Mass., 1984.

10. Ibid.

11. Ibid.

12. Walt Harrington, "Revenge of the Dupes," *The Washington Post Magazine*, 27 December 1987, pp. 17–21.

13. Magda Stouthamer-Loeber, "Lying as a Problem Behavior in Children: A Review," *Clinical Psychology Review* 6 (1986): 267–89.

14. These possibilities were raised by Magda Stouthamer-Loeber, ibid.

15. I found this quote in Thomas Lickona, *Raising Good Children* (New York: Bantam, 1983), p. 117.

16. See review by B. DePaulo and A. Jordan, "Age Changes in Deceiving and Detecting Deceit," in Robert S. Feldman, ed., *Development of Nonverbal Behavior in Children* (New York: Springer Verlag, 1982), pp. 151–80.

17. P. Ekman, *Telling Lies* (New York: W. W. Norton, 1985); P. Ekman and M. O'Sullivan, "Hazards in Detecting Deceit," in D. Raskin, ed., *Psychological Methods for Investigation and Evidence* (New York: Springer, in press); P. Ekman, "Why Lies Fail and What Behaviors Betray a Lie," in J. C. Yuille, ed., *Credibility Assessment—A Unified Theoretical and Research Perspective* (Dordrecht, The Netherlands: Kluwer Academic Publishers, in press); P. Ekman, W. V. Friesen, and M. O'Sullivan, "Smiles when Lying," *Journal of Personality and Social Psychology* 54 (1988): 414–20; P. Ekman and W. V. Friesen, "Felt, False and Miserable Smiles," *Journal of Nonverbal Behavior* 6 (1982): 238–52; P. Ekman and W. V. Friesen, "Detecting Deception from Body or Face," *Journal of Personality and Social Psychology* 29 (1974): 288–98; P. Ekman and W. V. Friesen, "Nonverbal Leakage and Clues to Deception," *Psychiatry* 32 (1969): 88–105.

18. R. S. Feldman, L. Jenkins, and O. Popoola, "Detection of Deception in Adults and Children via Facial Expressions," *Child Development* 50 (1979): 350–55 (quote from p. 351).

19. Nancy Lee Morency and Robert M. Krauss, "Children's Nonverbal Encoding and Decoding of Affect," in Feldman, *Development of Nonverbal Behavior in Children,* pp. 181–200.

20. William A. Shennum and Daphne B. Bugental "The Development of Control over Affective Expression," in ibid., pp. 101–21.

21. The quote is from Vasek's study.

22. For a discussion of the role of games in developing the skills needed in lying, see H. Sacks, "Everyone Has to Lie," in M. Sanches and B. G. Blount, eds., *Sociocultural Dimensions of Language Use* (New York: Academic Press, 1975), pp. 57–79.

23. J. G. deVilliers and P. A. deVilliers, *Language Acquisition* (Cambridge, Mass.: Harvard University Press, 1977); M. Shatz and R. Gelman, "The Development of Communication Skills: Modification in the Speech of Young Children as a Function of the Listener," *Monographs of the Society for Research in Child Development* 38 (1973): 1–38; see discussion by Vasek.

24. P. Ekman, G. Roper, and J. C. Hager, "Deliberate Facial Movement," *Child Development* 51 (1980): 886–91.

25. Michael F. Hoyt, "Secrets in Psychotherapy: Theoretical and Practical Considerations," *International Review of Psychoanalysis* 5, pt. 2 (1978): 223–41.

26. Ibid.

27. E. Turiel, "The Development of Social Concepts," in D. DePalma and J. Foley, eds., *Moral Development* (Hillsdale, N.J.: Lawrence Erlbaum, 1975). Cited by Damon.

28. I am grateful to Robert Coles, who in his very interesting book *The Moral Life of Children* (New York: Atlantic Monthly Press, 1986), reminded me of this statement by Anna Freud. It appeared in her book, *The Ego and the Mechanisms of Defense* (New York: International University Press, 1936).

29. For a brief statement, see L. Kohlberg, "Moral Stages and Moralization: The Cognitive-Developmental Approach," in Lickona, ed., *Moral Development and Behavior,* pp. 31–53.

30. See ref. 15 above.

31. Turiel, "The Development of Social Concepts," p. 155.

32. See J. R. Rest, "Morality," in P. H. Mussen, ed., *The Handbook of Child Psychology,* 4th ed. (New York: Wiley, 1983), vol. 3, pp. 556–629, for critical review. For a very interesting but quite different analysis of children's social judgment, see William Damon, *The Social World of the Child* (San Francisco: Jossey-Bass, 1977).

33. A. Blasi, "Bridging Moral Cognition and Oral Action: A Critical Review of the Literature," *Psychological Bulletin* 88 (1980): 1–45.

34. Carl I. Malinowski and Charles P. Smith, "Moral Reasoning and Moral Conduct: An Investigation Prompted by Kohlberg's Theory," *Journal of Personality and Social Psychology* 49 (1985): 1016–27.

CHAPTER FOUR

1. Lickona, *Raising Good Children,* p. 168.

CHAPTER FIVE

1. Kraut and Price, "Machiavellianism"; M. Lewis, "Parental Attitudes."

2. Bruno Bettelheim, *The Uses of Enchantment* (New York: Alfred A. Knopf, 1976), p. 9.

3. H. Hartshorne and M. A. May, *Studies in Deceit.*

4. See Rutter, Tizard, and Whitmore, eds., *Education, Health and Behavior*; Shepherd, Oppenheim, and Mitchell, *Childhood Behavior and Mental Health.*

5. *New York Times,* 24 January, 1987.

6. Ibid.

7. For a more complete discussion of Kohlberg's theory of the stages of moral development, see chapter 3.

8. Jodi Stewart, "The Story Behind 'Pig Boy,' " *San Francisco Chronicle,* 24 July 1988.

9. M. Hoffman and H. Saltzstein, "Parent Discipline and the Child's Moral Development," *Journal of Personality and Social Psychology* 5 (1967): p. 45.

10. As quoted in the *New York Times,* 18 June 1985, p. 23.

11. Ibid.

12. Ibid.

13. John Demos, *Past, Present and Personal* (New York: Oxford University Press, 1986), p. 46.

14. John Wesley, "Sermon on the Education of Children," in Philip Greven, ed., *Child Rearing Concepts, 1628–1861* (Itasca, Ill.: F. E. Peacock Publishers, Inc., 1973), p. 60.

15. Ibid., p. 61.

16. Ibid., p. 126.

17. Lenore Weitzman, *The Divorce Revolution* (New York: Free Press, 1985), p. xvii.

18. Judith S. Wallerstein and Joan Berlin Kelly, *Surviving the Breakup* (New York: Basic Books, 1980), pp. 33, 34.

19. Ibid., p. 60.

20. Ibid., p. 89.

21. In my recent book, *The Equality Trap* (New York: Simon and Schuster, 1988), I deal with the alarming popularity of joint custody. In some states it is imposed by the judge against the wishes of one parent. There is evidence that the effect on the children is negative.

22. S. Dornbush et al., "Single Parents, Extended Households and the Control of Adolescents," *Child Development* 56 (1985): 326–41.

23. Ibid., p. 333.

24. Mason, *The Equality Trap*, p. 18.

25. As quoted in ibid., p. 125.

26. Burton K. White, *The First Three Years of Life,* rev. ed. (New York: Prentice-Hall, 1985), p. 272.

CHAPTER SIX

1. Gail S. Goodman, "Child Witness: An Introduction," *Journal of Social Issues* 40 (1984): 28.

2. This is the opinion of California family court judges in Alameda and San Diego counties regarding the incidence of sexual abuse allegations in custody disputes in recent years. (Private interviews.)

3. Bill Girdner, "Out of the Mouths of Babes," *California Lawyer* 5 (June 1985): 59.

4. John Crewdson, *By Silence Betrayed* (Boston: Little, Brown, 1988), p. 127.

5. Bruno Bettelheim, *A Good Enough Parent* (New York: Knopf, 1987), p. 375.

6. Sigmund Freud, *Two Case Histories,* as quoted in S. Lindsay and M. Johnson, "Reality Monitoring and Suggestibility: Children's Ability to Discriminate Among Memories from Different Sources," in S. J. Ceci, M. P. Toglia, and D. F. Ross, eds., *Children's Eyewitness Memory* (New York: Springer-Verlag, 1987), p. 95.

7. J. Piaget, *Judgment and Reasoning in the Child,* in ibid., p. 98.

8. Lindsay and Johnson, "Reality Monitoring and Suggestibility," p. 101.

9. *New York Times,* 14 November 1987, p. 9.

10. Ibid.

11. Mason, *The Equality Trap,* p. 73. I have dealt at length with the subject of joint custody in this book.

12. As quoted in ibid., p. 174.

13. *New York Times,* 22 October 1986, p. 5.

14. *New York Times,* 31 March 1988, p. B13.

15. Melvin G. Goldzband, M.D., "Would Mommie Lie? An Inquiry into the Concept of Truth in Child Custody Litigation," unpublished manuscript, 1983.

16. Arthur H. Green, "True and False Allegations of Sexual Abuse in Child Custody Disputes," *Journal of the American Academy of Child Psychiatry* 25 (1986): 454.

17. *In re Sara,* 239 Cal. Rptr. 605.

18. *In the Matter of Cheryl H.,* 153 Cal. App.3d 1098, 200 Cal. Rptr. 789.

19. David Faust and Jay Ziskin, "The Expert Witness in Psychology and Psychiatry," *Science* 241 (July 1, 1988): 312.

20. "Incidence of Child Abuse in California," California Department of Justice Child Abuse Central Registry, Bureau of Criminal Statistics and Special Services, 1985, pp. 1–3.

21. Douglass J. Besharov, "Contending with Overblown Expectations," *Public Welfare* 45 (Winter 1987): 7–11.

22. Ibid., p. 10.

23. For a full discussion of the psychological research in this area, see Ceci, Toglia, and Ross, eds., *Children's Eyewitness Memory*; see also "The Child as Witness," *Journal of Social Sciences* 40, no. 2 (1984).

24. Maria Zagora, "Memory, Suggestibility, and Eyewitness Testimony in Children and Adults," in Ceci, Toglia, and Ross, eds., *Children's Eyewitness Memory,* p. 65.

25. Carole Cole and Elizabeth Loftus, "The Memory of Children," in ibid., pp. 195, 199.

26. Ceci, Ross, and Toglia, "Age Differences in Suggestibility," in ibid., p. 82.

27. B. Boat and M. Everson, paper presented at the Society for Research in Child Development Biennial Meeting, 1987.

28. M. King and J. Yuille, "Suggestibility and the Child Witness," in Ceci, Toglia, and Ross, eds., *Children's Eyewitness Memory,* p. 25.

29. D. Whitcomb, E. Shapiro, and L. Stellwagen, "When the Victim Is a Child: Issues for Judges and Prosecutors," U.S. Department of Justice, National Institute of Justice, 1981, pp. 69–73.

30. *Coy* v. *Iowa*, 108 S.Ct. 2798.

31. Ibid.

32. *New York Times,* 20 July 1988.

33. Gary B. Melton, "Procedural Reforms to Protect Victim/Witnesses in Sex Offense Proceedings," *Victimology: An Int'l. Journal* 5 (1980).

INDEX